HENRY'S FABULOUS MODEL A

by

Leslie R. Henry

Published and Copyrighted 1959

CLYMER PUBLICATIONS
World's largest publisher of books devoted exclusively to automobiles and motorcycles.
222 NO. VIRGIL AVENUE, LOS ANGELES, CALIFORNIA 90004

FOREWORD

This book on the FABULOUS MODEL A is unique in that it contains much data heretofore unpublished. The author, Leslie R. Henry, knows the Model A from stem to stern, all about the problems of the Model A owner, and what he needs to know about his car.

Much of the material appearing in this book has never been seen by the "A" owner. Few Ford dealers and very few laymen have beeen privileged to view the many interesting photos, charts and drawings, or read the text that appears in this volume. It is certainly the most complete book ever published on the Model A.

This book could have well been called "Edsel's Model A" for it was Henry's son, Edsel, who was responsible for the "A". When Model T sales in the mid-twenties started to dip and a new Ford model had to be developed, it was Edsel who sparked the idea for the design of Henry's new car — the "A". It took some "selling," you can be sure, to convince Henry Ford that the "A" was necessary. But, to regain top place in world sales of motor cars, the Ford Motor Company had to make a change — the "A" was "it."

Edsel was certain that the Model A would be an instant success — and it was. It had many features that appealed to car buyers. It was sturdy, powerful, economical and stylish for its day. Even without the prestige of the Ford name, it was a car that would have sold well by any manufacturer with a good sales organization.

How highly the Model A was regarded in its heydey, and is now, is a matter of record.

No other car built in the late twenties or the thirties is so much in demand and so popular with collectors and car enthusiasts as is the Model A. Thousands of restored Model A Fords still operate daily on highways of every state and in every foreign country. In our own United States hundreds of Clubs for Model A owners are in existence, and thousands of "A"s, beautifully restored to "as new" condition attract attention wherever they appear.

In recent years the Ford Motor Company has received thousands of letters urging them to again build the Model A. There's something about the Model A that catches the fancy of the enthusiast. The Model A will go down in history, along with the memories of the two great men who built it, Henry and Edsel Ford. The legend of the Model A remain in the hearts of car enthusiasts as long as even one remains in use anywhere.

I hope the readers enjoy this book as much as I did, both in reading the manuscript and in publishing it.

Floyd Clymer

TABLE OF CONTENTS

Foreword			2
Introduction			4
Acknowledgements			5
Dedication			6
CHAPTER	I	HENRY'S FABULOUS MODEL A	9
CHAPTER	II	"A" IS FOR FORD	15
CHAPTER	III	"X", THE UNKNOWN	23
CHAPTER	IV	DECIMATION AND DECISION	25
CHAPTER	V	NEW CREATION	29
CHAPTER	VI	DEBUT	35
CHAPTER	VII	EVOLUTION	39
CHAPTER	VIII	RESTORING MODEL A	61
CHAPTER	IX	HELPFUL HINTS	69
CHAPTER	X	ENGINE NUMBERS AND ASSEMBLY RECORDS	77
CHAPTER	XI	SPECIFICATIONS AND RESTORATION DATA	85
CHAPTER	XII	LOCATING MODEL A ENGINE TROUBLE	94
CHAPTER	XIII	PARTS SUPPLIERS AND SOURCES	98

ABOUT THE AUTHOR

An antiquarian and earnest collector of antique automobiles, LESLIE R. HENRY is best known as past president of the Antique Automobile Club of America and as an authoritative writer on the subject of antique cars. His "Ford Facts" is a regular department in the ANTIQUE AUTOMOBILE magazine, and his standard treatise, "The Ubiquitous Model T," is featured in Floyd Clymer's books, HENRY'S WONDERFUL MODEL T and MODEL T MEMORIES.

"Les" Henry, born while Model T was yet in colors other than BLACK, came to know both Model T and MODEL A at first hand and in more than a casual way. At the age of fourteen, he bought his first Model T Roadster, used and in pieces, with his entire bankroll of two dollars and learned to know the car the hard way—inside out! While still in college he acquired his first MODEL A, a well-used and incapacitated Town Sedan, which he alternately rebuilt and drove until his fianceé finally complained forcefully about its frightful height and antiquated appearance amid the more "streamlined" cars in the late 30s.

Mr. Henry's work in the field of petroleum products has been closely allied with the automotive world. Since 1940, he has been an engineer with the Atlantic Refining Company in Philadelphia, first in research and development, then in manufacturing. His interest in history and his love for old cars has kept him active in many of the national automotive organizations such as the Horseless Carriage Club of America, The Worldwide Old Car Club, the Model A Restorer's Club, and the Veteran Motor Car Club of America which has honored him with their "Certificate of Merit."

Unlike his secondary hobby of collecting antique American military firearms, antique automobiling is also the family hobby. His wife, Audrien, and his young son, Charlie, both enthusiastically share in the old car activities to such an extent that most week-ends and much vacation time are spent at "meets" and on cross-country tours arranged by the several clubs. So interested are the Henrys in this hobby, they literally brought it right into their home when they recently built their "garage with attached house" on a Newtown Square (Pa.) hillside—their antique cars occupy the entire basement!

For several years, Mr. Henry has been commentator for the Henry Ford Museum during their annual Old Car Festival at Greenfield Village in Dearborn, Michigan. And now, as technical vice president of the Antique Automobile Club of America, he is responsible for administering all technical aspects of this historical society which includes car classification, registration, dating, and authentication. His knowledge is not entirely academic, for four of his restored cars are AACA National First Prize Winners; a 1910 Maxwell Runabout, a 1915 Ford Touring, a 1928 Ford Phaeton, and a 1930 American Austin Roadster. Both his 1929 Ford Town Sedan (the "courting car") and his 1911 Chalmers Touring are National Second Prize Winners.

ABOUT THE ILLUSTRATIONS

Authenticity of restoration in the MODEL A Fords, as in all antique automobiles, is extremely important for preserving their historic value. Therefore, to insure authentic character of the illustrations, the author has chosen pictures from three sources in general:

First are the "official" photographs obtained through the courtesy of the Ford Motor Company showing actual scenes and cars of the MODEL A period.

Second are the photographs and illustrations reproduced from Ford publications and other literature contemporary with the MODEL A.

Third are the photographs of cars, mostly restored, in the hands of knowledgeable collectors today. The present owners' names and addresses are given, along with references to official positions they may hold in various recognized clubs or historical organizations, to indicate their genuine regard for the MODEL A and its authentic restoration. In this group of illustrations, frequent reference is made to the prize-winning qualities of the pictured cars as a further indication of their authenticity. One of the most valued awards is that of "National First Prize Winner" which is conferred only upon worthy, authentic, and nearly perfectly restored cars by the Antique Automobile Club of America, largest and oldest of the several automotive historical societies in the country.

LESLIE R. HENRY.

ACNOWLEDGEMENTS

Most of the material in this book, including much never before published, has been drawn from the records of the Ford Motor Company in Dearborn, Michigan. The author is deeply indebted to his many friends there—particularly to Henry E. Edmunds, Manager of the Research and Information Department, and to Owen Bombard—who made this material available and who gave much personal attention and help to him. An especially valuable source of information were the reminiscences of many knowledgeable Ford personnel of the MODEL A era—these were recorded as "oral history" by Owen Bombard.

Dr. Donald A. Shelley, Executive Director of the Henry Ford Museum and the Greenfield Village, and Alan R. Symonds, Curator of Transportation, not only lent their assistance but also provided opportunities for the author to examine pertinent museum pieces not on exhibition.

Thanks are due also to Kenneth Stauffer of Pottstown, Pa., photographer for the Antique Automobile Club of America, for many of the illustrations.

The author assumes full responsibility for any errors which may have insinuated themselves into the text, and for his interpretation of the facts made available to him by the Ford Motor Company.

LESLIE R. HENRY.

Photo courtesy Research & Information Dept., Ford Motor Company.

FIGURE 1.   EDSEL FORD 1893 - 1943

This book is dedicated to the memory of Edsel Ford, that quiet and circumscribed genius whose greatest works were, in his lifetime, eclipsed by the very name of Ford. As President of the Ford Motor Company, Edsel was the great internal force which brought the fabulous MODEL A into being thirty-one years ago. He was its principal instigator, protagonist, supervisor, and stylist. Perhaps this car, more than any other, should have borne his name in honor.

Leslie R. Henry

These photos show the front-end similarity between the "A" Ford (above) and the Lincoln (below). Both cars reflect the influence, design and styling ideas of Edsel Ford.

1928 SPORT COUPE   50-A

Various textured fabric tops impart some individuality to these Coupes. Even though the tops are rigid and the Landau irons but dummies; there is a real sporty air about this car.

1928 BUSINESS COUPE   54-A

The Business Coupe resembles the Sport Coupe except for lacking the Landau irons and rumble seat. Later in the year, an oval window was placed in the rear quarter panel.

CHAPTER I
HENRY'S FABULOUS MODEL A

Certainly MODEL A was a man's car in what was the beginning of a woman's market. By all precepts of the modern market researcher, MODEL A should have been a miserable failure in its first year. Instead it became a monument to the "Ford intuition."

Austere in style, masterful in design, economical to maintain, dependable in operation, MODEL A sprang into immediate leadership and acceptance by a nation already glutted with motor cars. It outsold, outperformed, and ultimately outlasted all competitors, and in its four brief years of production (1928-1931) earned a reputation as enviable as that of Rolls-Royce.

Born on the eve of prosperity, MODEL A thrived during the early depression years only to succumb amid the first throes of national recovery. Perhaps the delay in bringing out MODEL A had caused it to be misplaced in time, perhaps the new and vast program of building good highways had lessened the demand for so rugged a car, but most likely the telling stroke came from the dramatic change in buying habits attending the struggle for economic recovery. With automobiles, as with all commodities then, superficiality superseded functionality as the people demanded gaudier symbols of their gradually increasing economic victories.

MODEL A *was* a man's car, and there was no question in the mind of the man who once owned one that MODEL A was the best darned car ever built. It was! And the lucky man who now owns one believes that it still is! Not alone mere opinion, prejudiced by fond memories of its faithful service or by bright recollections of its youthsome errands, but MODEL A's own persistence bears this out.

How persistent is it? Of the original 5,000,000 MODEL A Fords produced in all the world, there are actually 80,000 registered for daily use in Pennsylvania alone, and there are estimated at least 920,000 registered in all the United States. To these, and to the thousands more already in the hands of automobile collectors, are being added each year hundreds of MODEL A Fords saved from the open hearths which have long since melted down the lesser breeds.

What other thirty year old car in such numbers still performs routine chores for oldsters or furnishes lively sport for youngsters? What other aged car gives its engine so generously to farm and industrial service;* its body, engine, and chassis so universally to dirt track racers and highway hot rods? What other car of any age so thoroughly outjeeps the Jeep on the beaches (SEE FIG. 85), in the swamps, in the backwoods, in the hinterland? None. For none that was sleeker, smoother, softer, costlier had the simplicity, reliability, stamina, and durability that made MODEL A, of all, the best.

NOTE: *Perhaps the greatest tribute to the excellence of design and stamina of MODEL A comes indirectly from the Soviet Army. Their military equivalent of the U.S. Jeep, which they produced for use in World War II and which IS STILL BEING PRODUCED in Russia in their original Ford factory, is the MODEL A Ford! Most details of the 1929 MODEL A are quite apparent except for the change in springing to accommodate the four-wheel drive and the modified body – even the old, familiar dash panel and fuel tank is retained! Col. G. B. Jarrett, who has tested these captured Soviet "jeeps" at the Aberdeen Proving Ground, reports them to be every bit as good as the U.S. Jeep.*

It is interesting to note also that the Bantam Car Company of Butler, Pennsylvania – not Willys – originated and designed the U.S. Jeep in 1938; their Jeep No. 1 is in the Smithsonian Institution on display.

Never before nor since had such a low priced car been built to such high standards of quality. Typical of the sturdy design and materials in MODEL A were the universal joint and the wheel bearings. Unchanged for more than twenty years, these parts still adequately served for 1948 Fords and Mercurys weighing half again as much as MODEL A and having nearly triple its power.

MODEL A's popularity is as enduring as the car itself. And this very durability which makes the car still available also inspires confidence to continue it in use despite its age. Popularity stems partly from its sentimental value to many of us who came to know and use it during our school days before World War II. There are those of us yet who, from pure sentimentality, take keen delight in hearing MODEL A's unique automotive sounds—the metallic ring and grind of the starter; the cheery hiss of the carburetor; the low whine of the spur geared transmission; the sharp pup-pup-pup-pup of the exhaust; the distinctive "ah-ooga" of its Sparton horn.

Many of us are finding a newly awakened interest in MODEL A; Michigan's Governor G. Mennen Williams, who learned to drive in a MODEL A, now takes delight in driving those owned and restored by his brother, Dick. And AACA's past President T. Clarence Marshall, who has been a Stanley and Packard advocate most of his life, has restored a 1929 MODEL A Phaeton for his personal use and for display in his Stanley Steamer Museum at Yorklyn, Delaware. William E. Swigart, another AACA past president, is preparing a MODEL A Roadster for himself and his Swigart Museum at Huntington, Pennsylvania. William Klein, chocolate manufacturer in Elizabethtown, Pennsylvania, proudly displays his restored MODEL A Phaeton amid his famous collection of antique and modern Bentley cars.

Even the Thompson Products Auto Museum in Cleveland, Ohio, which considers only cars at least thirty-five years old as "antique," now has a MODEL A Ford on hand for restoration. And William Pollock, President of AACA, is about to restore a MODEL A for his private museum in Pottstown, Pennsylvania, while Dr. Wendell H. Stadle, President of VMCCA, has already restored a 1928 Ford Phaeton for his collection of fine cars in Battle Creek, Michigan.

Others of us, recognizing a good thing when we had it, maintained our personal or family MODEL A with loving care these many years—not the least of whom are Mrs. E. Paul duPont, New York's Governor Nelson A. Rockefeller, and ex-Governor W. Averell Harriman (SEE FIGS. 6, 7, 8). And, not to be outdone by individual owners, the United States Post Office, in mountainous Colorado Springs, maintains some of their original MODEL A trucks in daily mail service along with their new trucks!

During the Model A era the Ford engine was used for variety of applications including yard locomotives, industrial handling equipment, stationary and portable power units, and marine boat uses but the most startling use was in the airplane. Several companies and individuals designed and built airplanes using the Ford Model A engine. A western manufacturer built what was called the Barling monoplane using a modified Ford A engine. Modifications included larger valves, valve ports and manifold; force feed lubrication; special carburetor and crankshaft thrust bearing. The engine developed 59 HP at 2300 rpm and it was said these planes could climb from an altitude of 2000 feet to 3000 feet in 1½ minutes.

Photo courtesy Research & Information Dept., Ford Motor Company.

FIGURE 4.   HENRY FORD, EDSEL FORD, AND "BABY LINCOLN"

The Fords, father and son, could well be pleased with this stylish Fordor Sedan, introduced in the Ford line late in 1928 after the first flood of orders had been filled and the assembly line had settled down to a smooth routine of production.

Probably the best looking of all their closed models, the Fordor Sedan, and later the Town Sedan, had the cowl fuel tank concealed under the smoother body shell; all other 1928-29 Fords had the "coupe pillar" and the tank exposed as a part of the body itself. The fabric covered rear panel and the extension of the body moulding across the cowl and engine hood gave an air of "class" to the Sedans.

Note the little cylindrical tail lamp, characteristic of the 1928 Fords.

Photo by Kenneth Stauffer, AACA Photographer.

FIGURE 5.   THIRTY YEARS ON THE ROAD!

This 1929 Town Sedan, 155A, was in continuous use for 96,000 miles by its original owner until 1957 when the author purchased it "for sentimental reasons" and completely rebuilt it to like-new condition.

"I like it because it is *exactly* identical to my first MODEL A which I drove during college and after, until my fiance', Audie, objected to riding in 'that old car' with me. Today she is proud to *drive it*—with or without me!"

There are other practical aspects of MODEL A's popularity. In the phaeton or roadster body, it is still the poor man's sport car with its unusual combination of classically sporty lines, crash gearbox, relatively rapid acceleration, handling ease, quick cornering, and its insistent urge to *go!*

SCIENCE AND MECHANICS magazine ran controlled performance tests in 1956 on a worn 1930 Ford Roadster (*not* the fastest of the MODEL As!) and found its speed at the end of a quarter mile from a standing start was 50 MPH in 27.6 seconds. This was the average of several two-way runs; the one best time was 0-50 MPH in 24.6 seconds!

MODEL A's honest claim to sports car characteristics is well supported by performance trials for the recent Anglo-American Vintage Car Rally. On the hill climb in Reading, Pennsylvania on October 19, 1956, for instance, two MODEL A Phaetons held their own against the formidable competition of two recognized contemporary sports cars; a MercerRaceabout and a duPont Speedster. This hill, known as Duryea Drive from the time Charles A. Duryea tested his cars there during 1900 to 1907, rises sharply 800 feet in 2½ miles of roadway with three hairpin turns and one S-turn followed by a short, straight run to the summit. It is considered a real challenge even to modern sports cars.

Just how good MODEL A proved to be on the climb is best shown in the table below which gives the best time made by each of the four cars selected for comparison:

ANGLO-AMERICAN VINTAGE CAR RALLY TRIALS
HILL CLIMB — 1956
(Sponsored by the Veteran Motor Car Club of America)

Year	Car	H.P.	Driver-Owner	Time	Photo
1922	Mercer Raceabout	73	Ralph Buckley	230.39	Fig.10
1928	FORD Phaeton	40	Robert Grier*	235.58	Fig.11
1929	duPont Speedster	140	Stanley Smith	249.31	Fig.12
1928	FORD Phaeton	40	Leslie Henry	249.49	Fig.13
1957	Oldsmobile "88"	277		200	

(Unofficial run for comparison with a modern car)
*Owner—Long Island Automotive Museum, Southhampton, N.Y. (Henry Austin Clark, Jr.)

And, in any body type, MODEL A is the automobile collector's joy. It is antiquated in appearance, inexpensive to buy and to restore, simple to repair, easy to find parts for, fast on the road, and worthy of prideful ownership. Indeed, MODEL A wins new devotees every day. And so great is its growing new popularity that Scott Bailey, editor of the ANTIQUE AUTOMOBILE, estimates there will be 17,000 *restored* MODEL A Fords in the hands of collectors by 1961. Already there are several clubs (SEE PAGE 00) devoted exclusively to the restoration and preservation of MODEL A, and the oldest and largest automotive historical society in America, the Antique Automobile Club of America, accords MODEL A its own classification for judging and competition of antique cars.

Even today MODEL A has aesthetic appeal, with all its antique appearance, for there is real beauty of form in its functional simplicity and trimness. It has neither forward look nor backward look, and there is nowhere about it the slightest suggestion of wings, fins, jets, nor rockets. MODEL A has a priceless ingredient—integrity.

MODEL A is unique today—it honestly looks like an automobile!

FIGURE 6. "I COULD NEVER PART WITH IT!"

So says Mrs. duPont, of Montchanin, Delaware.

The late E. Paul duPont, himself designer and manufacturer of the classic duPont automobiles, chose this MODEL A Phaeton as a present for his wife in 1929. That Mrs. Jean Kane Faulke duPont still cherishes it, frequently uses it, and proudly exhibits it today at AACA Meets is a real tribute to the lasting appeal and quality of MODEL A.

Her Ford Phaeton 35-A, photographed near the Water Wheel House at Squirrel Hill in 1958, still has the original top boot and fabric-covered trunk, with its set of fitted luggage, in service. It has been repainted once; original color is Andalusite blue body, black fenders, and blue grained upholstery.

By way of contrast, see one of Mr. duPont's automotive creations shown in Fig. 12.

Photo courtesy LIFE Magazine.

FIGURE 7A. MODEL A AND THE GOVERNOR.

New York's new Governor, Nelson A. Rockefeller, has carefully maintained this 1931 Ford Phaeton in original condition and still enjoys driving it at his summer estate at Seal Harbor, Maine. Governor Rockefeller appears here at the wheel with wife, Tod, sons, daughter-in-law, and grandchildren around him.

This photograph and the MODEL A figured prominently in Rockefeller's 1958 campaign for the governorship.

LETTERS TO THE EDITORS

LIFE Magazine.

Sirs:

As a member of the Detroit chapter of the Model "A" Restorers Club, I could not help noticing Rockefeller's "1933 Ford." If I am not mistaken, the car is actually a 1930 or 1931 Model "A." The car appears to have a vacuum type windshield wiper which would indicate that it was built between June 1930 and October 1931.

STEWART A. MURRAY

Detroit, Mich.

● "It's a 1931 Model A, all right," says Mr. Rockefeller. "I bought it from my brother David in 1933. It still runs beautifully."—ED.

ROCKEFELLER AND HIS 1931 MODEL A

FIGURE 7B.

Photo courtesy New York State Dept. of Commerce.

FIGURE 8. MODEL A AND THE GOVERNORS.

Not to be outdone by his gubernatorial rival, Rockefeller, New York's Governor W. Averell Harriman proudly campaigned in his own 1929 MODEL A Ford Roadster. Here Robert Fisk, driver, and the Governor's other grandchildren wait while he shakes hands and chats with New Jersey's Governor Robert Meyner.

None but MODEL A, the American people's car, could serve so well in this campaign to link two wealthy candidates with the American people themselves.

Averell Harriman has the distinction of being the first purchaser of a MODEL A in New York City, December 2, 1927!

Photo by William T. Browne, Chatham, N. J.

FIGURE 9. A "NOBLE" FORD — 1929 STATION WAGON.

Owned by Henry B. Gilbert, Bowmansdale, Pa.
Restored by the Snyder brothers, Mt. Joy, Pa.

Once the chauffeur-driven car preferred by Lady Virginia Thornton, widow of Sir Henry Thornton who was President of the Canadian National Railway before his death, this Station Wagon is the current favorite of young and old in the Gilbert family today.

Though rarer, the Station Wagons are closely following the Phaetons and Roadsters in current popularity. This model 150-A, engine number A1494547, is one of the very few actually assembled in the Ford plant; it shows the removable rear seat with the two folding center seats.

Mr. Gilbert's car is one of the finest of authentic restorations in recent years; it was AACA National First Prize Winner at Hershey, and recipient of the coveted Thompson Products Museum Award for the best restoration of any car of a make still in production today.

Photo courtesy Ralph Buckley.

FIGURE 10. MIGHTY MERCER RACEABOUT — 1922.

Owned and restored by Ralph Buckley, Absecon, N. J.

A king of the road in its day, the popular Mercer sports car could run 90 miles per hour with ease and outmaneuver most other cars on the curves.

This Raceabout, number 19350, has won many prizes in AACA and VMCCA, including the coveted AACA "Mercer Award." Ralph Buckley, a past Director of AACA, drove it in the winning team of American cars in the 1957 Anglo-American Vintage Car Rally. In the preliminary Duryea Drive hill climb it easily beat the younger duPont and the MODEL A Fords with a time of 230.39 seconds.

CHAPTER II
"A" IS FOR FORD

First there was Henry Ford—farmer, mechanic*, intuitive genius, rugged individualist, industrial giant, presidential candidate, antiquary, and the last billionaire! Through his life's work he attained greatness that well befitted him, and upon him was thrust greatness that sometimes taxed his capacities for such. A common man with uncommon attributes, Henry Ford enjoyed tremendous popularity both as a public benefactor and as an individual. In the eyes of the public his achievements attested to his greatness, his foibles to his humanness—and therein lay his popular appeal. When he moved, the world watched; when he spoke the world listened—in agreement or not! His successes were stupendous; his mistakes appalling, and there was little in between. He once said, "I never made a mistake; but I have made some unsuccessful experiments." This was a terminological inexactitude.

But withal, he lived a relatively simple life in the four thousand acre seclusion of "Fair Lane" in Dearborn, shunning the more ostentatious social and civic life of the wealthy in Detroit and Grosse Point. Even his past-times were simple—he liked folk dancing, ice skating, walking, and playing with his grandchildren at the residency. Most of all, he enjoyed the informal camping trips across country with his friends Thomas Edison, Harvey Firestone, and John Burroughs, the naturalist.

To Henry Ford success came late, though bountifully. For years it had seemed almost beyond reach as first his Detroit Automobile Company of 1900, and then his Henry Ford Automobile Company of 1902 went under with scarcely a ripple on the surface of America's six-year-old automobile industry. Ford at forty was still a mechanic of some experience but no wealth when he founded his third—and finally successful—automobile manufactory, the Ford Motor Company. Genius and experience were his only capital, his only contribution to that infant company when incorporated on June 16, 1903. For his talents, Henry Ford received initially 255 of the original 1,000 shares of stock, as did his partner, Alexander Malcomson.

Contributions in the form of cash, shop space, materials, and machine shop work came from others who received the remainder of the stock. For example, the Dodge brothers, John and Horace, together received a one-tenth interest in the company for building engines and "running gear" for Ford in their own shop. Out of their 100 shares, the Dodge brothers eventually drew $35,000,000. And, within twenty years, Henry Ford came to own *all* the stock and drew three times that sum as profit annually—but not in 1903, not by any means!

Of course, the first car built by the Ford Motor Company was designated "Model A," a car all but forgotten by all collectors today. As an automobile it was good enough to meet competition, which meant that it was as good as the 89 competitors which survived in 1903, and better than the 134 which did not. Model A distinguished itself primarily by putting the Ford Motor Company on its feet in the first three months of its corporate life, and by firmly establishing the company by the end of its first year—but not without struggle on the part of all concerned.

*Henry Ford built his first automobile in 1896—(See Fig. 14).

With an actual subscribed capital of only $28,500 at hand, the company verged on bankruptcy for two months. The method of operating then was interesting but not unusual. The company would purchase materials on a thirty-day cash basis; build as many cars as possible in that time; then convert them to cash by immediate local sale, or on sight drafts on bills of lading for distant purchasers. Thus they obtained the working capital to meet the thirty-day bills, the rent, and the payroll. Anything left was profit to be put back into the growing business.

Thus, between June and September, the Ford Motor Company built 150 Model As, sold them for about $150,000, and made a profit of $36,000—which was considerably more than the subscribed capital. Success was on the way!

In appearance, Model A was much like other "horseless carriages" of its day—under the driver's seat was a two-cylinder engine, facing fore and aft. Its transmission shaft bearings, mounted on the frame side rails, were in a constant state of misalignment as the car twisted and bounced over rough roads. The radiator was nothing more than several rows of finned copper tubing under the floorboards above the front axle. Final drive was by a single chain to the rear wheels. An unusual feature of the Model A was its steering wheel—most other cars of that period were still guided by tillers, though selling for more than the Ford's $950 price.

Except for its having only one cylinder, the 1903 Cadillac (SEE FIG. 16) closely resembled the Model A Ford (SEE FIG. 15) but sold for $50 less! This similarity is understandable because the bodies were not only built by the same maker, but the designers of these two cars, Henry Leland and Henry Ford, had been associated in the Henry Ford Automobile Company. In general they thought alike, but they had strong differences of opinion about methods, and so parted, each to form his own company. Parenthetically, it is interesting to note that Henry Leland went on to build another fine and famous automobile, the Lincoln, which, in 1922, came into the hands of Ford. Thus Henry Leland began and ended his automotive work in association with—and still in disagreement with—Henry Ford!

But even as success began to smile upon the young Ford company, there appeared a black cloud in the form of the Selden Patent suit to blot out that smile. This patent was generally considered to be a broad one covering the application of an internal combustion "hydrocarbon engine" to propelling a road vehicle. The patent was owned and controlled by the Electric Vehicle Company for the Association of Licensed Automobile Manufacturers (A.L.A.M.) which exercised monopolistic control over the automobile industry through their power to grant *or to deny* licenses for the manufacture of automobiles. One by one, manufacturers fell into line, applying to A.L.A.M. for licenses. Henry Ford made unofficial inquiry about obtaining a license in 1903 and was told that his "organization was nothing more than an assemblage plant" and so not qualified as a manufacturer, but others, already licensed, were no different. Later, Ford refused to deal with the A.L.A.M.

Photo courtesy Long Island Automotive Museum.

FIGURE 11. FASTEST FORD PHAETON — EARLY 1928.

From Henry Austin Clark's Long Island Automotive Museum, Southampton, N.Y.

Perfectly restored to original condition and Arabian Sand color, this MODEL A is greatly prized by Mr. Clark who is a past President of the Veteran Motor Car Club of America. Bob Grier drove this 35-A Phaeton on the winning American team in the 1957 Anglo-American Vintage Car Rally; in preliminary trials it made the 2½ mile Duryea Drive hill climb in 235.58 seconds and touched up to 75 miles per hour on the road.

The absence of outside door handles is a mark of the early 1928 Ford; other characteristics are the left side hand brake, the multiple disc clutch, and the smaller hub caps. Note the original type Firestone tires.

Photo by Stanley Smith.

FIGURE 12. DASHING DUPONT SPEEDSTER — 1929.

Owned and restored by Stanley B. Smith, State College, Pa.

This strikingly masculine looking sports car was designed and manufactured by the late E. Paul duPont, a past director and benefactor of AACA.

It was one of the winning team of American cars on the 1957 Anglo-American Vintage Car Rally; and piloted by Stanley Smith, who is a Vice President of the Antique Automobile Club of America, it was a formidable adversary for the two MODEL A Fords in the preliminary trials. Capable of speeds above 100 miles per hour, this duPont ran the Duryea Drive hill climb in 249.31 seconds.

Photo courtesy Len Millhauser, Reading, Pa.

FIGURE 13. FAMOUS FORD PHAETON — LATE 1928.

Owned and restored by Leslie R. Henry, Newtown Square, Pa.

A repeated national First Prize Winner in AACA and MARC, this car was runner-up for the 1957 Anglo-American Vintage Car Cally. In preliminary trials it made the 2½ mile Duryea Drive hill climb in 249.49 seconds; attained 72 miles per hour on the road.

While definitely a 1928 Ford, its engine number A650674 and its original single disc clutch mark it as one of the latest. The upholstery is still the 1928 brown, steering wheel is red, and color is Arabian Sand with Seal Brown trim. Note the outside door handles and the original type Firestone tires. Mr. Henry, a past President of the Antique Automobile Club of America, considers this his favorite car.

Photo courtesy Research & Information Dept., Ford Motor Company.

FIGURE 14. FORD'S FIRST . . . 1896.

Henry Ford's first car, a "quadricycle," is preserved in running order by the Henry Ford Museum in Dearborn, Michigan. Except for the few inevitable changes made by Henry Ford while still experimenting with it, the car is essentially the same now as the day he first drove it — June 4, 1896.

Truly a pioneer, Henry Ford was one of the first half-dozen experimenters — or "tinkerers" — with self-propelled vehicles in America. He alone rose to complete world dominance in automobile production with his product — the FORD.

"If you buy a Ford, you buy a lawsuit," the A.L.A.M. then advertised. And Ford countered in his advertisements: "Notice to dealers, agents, importers, and users of gasolene automobiles: we will protect you against any prosecution for alleged infringements of the Selden Patent. The Selden Patent is not a broad one, and if it were it is anticipated. It does not cover a practicable machine, no practicable machine can be made from it and never was so far as we can ascertain. It relates to a form of carriage called a FORE CARRIAGE. None of that type has ever been in use, all have been failures. No court in the United States has ever decided in favor of the patent on the merits of the case, all it has ever done was to record a prior agreement between the parties."

Thus began an eight-year legal battle between Ford, the manufacturer, and A.L.A.M., the "big trust"—a battle from which Henry Ford emerged victor and popular hero as a "trust buster." The supreme court had finally ruled, in 1911, that while the Selden Patent was indeed valid, it did not apply to the type of automobile built by Ford —or by any other manufacturer in the United States!

By 1904, Ford had responsible dealers all over the country; notable among them was the first, John Wanamaker, in New York and Philadelphia. For the first time in the industry, mechanics were employed to visit the Ford agencies to instruct them on the "machines," and to help them deal with crippled cars. The policy became the cornerstone of the since famous Ford service, and contributed greatly to the success of the Ford Motor Company right from the beginning.

For the 1905 season, Ford brought out his Model B, a four cylinder touring car priced at $2,000 and his Model C, another two cylinder car priced the same as the former Model A—$950. These were great improvements over the Model A for they followed the more advanced European principles. The engine of Model B had been moved from its inaccessible position under the seat and mounted up front, under a hood, with the radiator occupying the front part of the hood. The Model C was even more novel in that the rear seat, or "tonneau" was reached through side doors rather than by one door in the rear as was common to all other cars. Today, the "rear entrance tonneau" survives only in the ambulance and the hearse!

Still experimenting with size, design, and price, Ford added the four cylinder Model F to the line at $1,200. He followed with the enormous six cylinder Model K costing $2,800 in 1906 through 1908 (SEE FIG. 17). This car had an engine more suited to racing than to touring, and had a two-speed planetary transmission not particularly suited to either. At the same time, he tried the little four cylinder cars, Models N, R, and S. This was in accord with the profound belief in the industry that no manufacturer could survive by concentrating on a single model—that he must offer a choice and make annual changes.*

But Model K's impact on the Ford Company was deep and lasting because of its effect on Henry Ford. It turned him with certainty to producing one small, simple, low-priced car for the masses, and it turned him irrevocably from building a six cylinder car as long as he dominated the company. Indeed, when Henry Ford finally abandoned the four cylinder engine for his cars he went directly to his revolutionary en bloc V-8 engine. He agreed with Harry Miller, Indianapolis race car builder, who said, "there's no excuse for a six; it has all the engineering difficulties of an eight with none of its advantages."

*This is a popular belief among automobile manufacturers even today—excepting those who manufacture the German Volkswagen, standardized in 1938, and the Rambler American, standardized in 1950.

Now, after five years of trial and experiment with multiple models, Henry Ford realized that his dream of producing a universal car could materialize only by standardizing on one design, then mass producing it— making it cheaper even as he had made it better. His announcement, in 1908, that thereafter the Ford Motor Company would produce only one model car not only startled the automobile world, but evoked dire predictions of his failure. But Henry Ford then owned 58% of the company and could freely follow his intuition. As if to answer his critics, he said:

"I will build a motor car for the great multitude. It will be large enough for the family but small enough for the individual to run and care for. It will be constructed of the best materials, by the best men to be hired, after the simplest designs that modern engineering can devise. But it will be so low in price that no man making a good salary will be unable to own one—and enjoy with his family the blessing of hours of pleasure in God's great open spaces."

He did.

And then there was Model T—Henry made it and it made Henry. His reputation was built almost entirely on the Model T. It was all that Henry Ford had made it and had expected of it—and more. It was not merely another car—it was a national institution. It was not merely a part of the American scene—it *was* the American scene! As a car it was purely utilitarian: unquestionably ugly, uncompromisingly erect, funereally drab, Model T combined the web footedness of the duck with the agility of the mountain goat. It could go anywhere—except in society! Half affectionately and half derisively called "Tin Lizzie," it was the constant butt of jokes. But even those who ridiculed it, laughed at it, and joked about it respected it for the service it rendered and the revolution it wrought. Henry Ford was facetiously reported to have two assembly lines—one for the cars and one for the jokes!

The jokes were as standardized as the car, and standardization of the car was the key to success. In nearly twenty years, Henry Ford produced more than 15,000,000 Model Ts without any basic change in design—this *was* mass production; this was vindication of his ideas and methods—his dream materialized.

In 1914 and 1915, Henry Ford even standardized on one color—black—for his cars (SEE FIG. 14), not because of mere whim, but because he found that black paint covered well with only two coats (colors needed seven coats, including varnish) and so speeded up production. This was the time when he again startled the world with his eight-hour, five-dollar minimum work day. Again the automobile industry, then paying but half that wage, predicted failure for Ford. But Ford didn't fail—he pulled another world beater—he declared a $50 profit-sharing refund to every Ford purchaser during the year ending August 1, 1915! The black paint, the simplifications in the 1915 design, and the faster work required of his better-paid labor helped make all this possible. The mark of Henry was upon the Ford—the mark of the Ford was upon the land—and a new doctrine for the world was "Fordismus."

In 1917, Henry Ford further enhanced his popularity when he contested the stockholders' suit, led by the Dodge brothers, seeking to force him to stop building his new River Rouge works, to stop sharing profits with the public, and to pay that money to the company's stockholders instead. Henry Ford appeared to the public then as the champion of profit-sharing and expansion of business for greater employment and lower product prices. He lost the suit in 1919, but immediately countered with a veiled move to withdraw from the Ford Motor Company, and he named his son, Edsel, as President. He did not deny rumors that the new company, Henry Ford & Son, organized to manufacture Fordson tractors, would produce cars in competition with the Ford Motor Company.

Since his stockholders wanted only to share his profits, not compete with him, they readily sold out to Henry Ford for $105,821,000. With the cash dividend and interest ordered by the court, the total cost to Henry Ford for complete ownership of his company was $126,633,000—some sum!

But now, in 1919, he personally wielded industrial power such as no man had ever possessed before—not even John D. Rockefeller nor J. P. Morgan ever controlled as much as one-third of *their* respective organizations, Standard Oil and United States Steel Corporation. Yet Henry Ford had given only his title, *not his power*, to Edsel; Henry Ford still ran the Ford Motor Company.

Furthermore, Henry Ford pushed rapidly ahead with the construction of the Rouge works, and by 1920 had put about $60,453,000 into that plant (SEE FIG. 24). With such expenditures, Ford was in no better position financially than most other manufacturers when the depression of 1920 came. He pulled through with the financial help of his dealers upon whom he loaded Model Ts on sight drafts, for which they had to borrow heavily—sometimes even mortgaging their homes—in order to retain their dealerships. Their franchises had been quite profitable in the past and promised to be so again if only they could weather out the depression. The dealers who thus helped finance the Ford Motor Company had a rough time for a while, but profited in the end.

By 1924, Model T had reached its zenith but its end was even then in sight. Others saw it clearly, but Henry Ford saw it not; neither would he then listen to his son, Edsel, nor to others in his organization who were "faithless" enough to speak of it. The "great multitude," Mr. Ford thought, was not interested in change nor in fashions; it did not care about pretty lines nor about colors in a car: it wanted something useful to drive in town or country, something that would meet any road conditions, something that took no thought to drive, no expense to maintain, no special skill to repair.

"Why should I change my Model T," Mr. Ford would say, "when I can't make as many as I can sell now?" And he believed the multitude would go on wanting his Model T in the future—this was part of the doctrine of "Fordismus."

It was undoubtedly Edsel Ford, titular head of the Ford Motor Company, who finally convinced Henry Ford, absolute autocrat of the company, that what the multitude wanted was a Ford car alright—but *not* the Model T! So, in June of 1927, with the stamping of number 15,458,781 on an engine block, the end came for Model T. Henry Ford had at last bowed to the inevitable, turned his back on the past, banished "Model T thinking" from his organization, retooled his Rouge plant, and started afresh.

And then came MODEL A—not a revamped Model T, but an entirely new car, designed and created in less than a year expressly for interminable mass production. It was a monument to the brilliant work of Edsel Ford, Henry Ford, and the many Ford engineers. To indicate how completely it would sweep away all previous models with its newness it was named "MODEL A." It was to be the beginning of a new dynasty of Ford cars.

Never the butt of jokes, MODEL A was greeted with the enthusiasm and held in esteem. "Henry made a lady out of Lizzie" was the closest people ever came to joking about this car—many called it the "Baby Lincoln," in recognition of its qualities and its appearance (SEE FIGS. 2 AND 3).

You may call it "A MODEL" in Dixie or "MODEL A" up north, as you will, but everywhere everyone knows what you mean—"A" is for Ford!

Photo courtesy The Strong Auto Collection.

FIGURE 15. HENRY FORD'S 1903 MODEL A

While the fame of this 1903 Model A Ford has been eclipsed by that of the fabulous MODEL A which came 25 years later, it was a car good enough to establish the infant Ford Motor Company firmly during the first year of its manufacture. Priced then at $950, it offered twice as many cylinders as its one-cylinder competitor, Cadillac, which sold for $50 less! Both these cars looked alike (see Fig. 16), partly because both had bodies made by the same builder and both had the same *new* feature—a steering wheel!

This Model A rear-entrance Tonneau Ford is one of the complete collection of early Fords, including the rare Model F, owned by Sidney Strong of Atwater, Minnesota. Mr. Strong was formerly a director of the AACA. The Strong Motor Company was one of the first Ford agencies.

Mr. and Mrs. Strong at present have five of the later MODEL A's, one of which they have *preserved* in showroom condition, and all of which they still enjoy driving.

FIGURE 16. HENRY LELAND'S 1903 CADILLAC.

The 1903 Cadillac bore a striking resemblance to the 1903 Ford (see Fig. 15) for its designer, Henry Leland, had been associated with Henry Ford in the short-lived Henry Ford Automobile Company and, of course, both men were still thinking along the same lines.

Both the Cadilalc and the Ford departed from the "tiller" this year and boasted of something new—a steering wheel! Both cars had the same small 28 x 3 tires and both had finned tube radiators hung under the front of the body.

The 8 h.p., one-cylinder engine under the seat caused the Cadillac to pulsate alarmingly and repeatedly vibrated the fenders off their brackets! But Cadillac ran well and far, and is one of the few pioneers still in business today.

The rear-entrance Tonneau Cadillac pictured here was owned and restored by William Fleming, Wycomb, Pa., and has been a frequent First Prize winner in the AACA and VMCCA.

Photo courtesy "Antique Automobile" magazine.

FIGURE 17. MODEL K — THE FORD "SIX" OF 1906.

Owned and restored by Elmer K. Bemis, Brattleboro, Vt.

Always considered "unsatisfactory" by its builder, Henry Ford, this 1906 Model K performed beautifully (except for a gear repair) for Mr. and Mrs. Bemis on the 1954 VMCCA "Ango-American Vintage Car Rally" in England. It has since successfully completed several "Glidden Tours" of antique cars, and is pictured here at the Firestone stop on the 1955 AACA Glidden Tour in Canada.

The Model K had a six-cylinder engine of 40 horsepower; had a two-speed planetary transmission similar to the Model T; and had a lasting effect on the Ford Motor Company through Henry Ford's subsequent prejudice against *all* six-cylinder cars.

Photo courtesy Don McCray, Chicago, Ill.

FIGURE 18. "TIN LIZZIE," THE UNIVERSAL CAR.

In 1915 Henry Ford produced 400,000 of these angular, box-like Tin Lizzies "in any color you wanted so long as it was black!" Such high volume of sales then enabled him to raise wages, share profits, and lower prices of the subsequent models which were further improved.

The author and his wife, Audrien Henry, appear here with their 1915 Ford Touring car, number 762316, which won the Ford Motor Company Trophy for the best Model T on the 1950 International Glidden Tour.

Photo courtesy Research and Information Dept., Ford Motor Company.

**FIGURE 19. EXPERIMENTAL FORD X-8 ENGINE
(1922 to 1926)**

This radical X-8 engine was Henry Ford's idea for the successor to Model T. One such engine was road tested. Note the finned cylinders cast in pairs, the "L" arrangement of the valves operated by two camshafts, and the twin flywheel fans for cooling. Also visible are the twin exhaust manifolds. Other unusual features of this engine are steel pistons and roller bearings for the crankshaft. Bore and stroke are 3⅜" x 4"; displacement is 286 cu. in.

CHAPTER III
"X", THE UNKNOWN

Henry Ford, the individual, was waxing expansive in 1922; not only had he captured a large part of the world's tractor market and taken over the Lincoln plant and production, but he was already thinking of an ultimate successor for his prodigious baby, Model T. And, since Model T from its very inception was immutable, its successor could never merely evolve from it but must suddenly appear as a completely new and remarkably revolutionary car—a creation distinctive of Henry Ford.

As undisputed leader in the automotive world, Henry Ford scorned conventionality and lauded originality. Always he sought the unusual for expression of his works as if thereby to demonstrate that he, the leader, did not "imitate others." Consequently, he conceived the X-8 car as a totally unique design intended one day to supplant Model T. And Henry Ford was very positive that he alone would name that day.

His X engine was to consist of four pairs of cylinders arranged around a central crankshaft; four cylinders up and four down, in the form of the letter "X." (SEE FIG. 19). This design particularly appealed to him because of its novelty, its perfect balance, and its compactness—it could be easily fitted into a short wheelbase car such as his Model T.

Under his direction, some preliminary design work was done on the X engine by Allan Horton before he left in 1924. Then the project was put in the capable hands of Eugene J. Farkas who, with Harold E. Hicks and a small group from Ford Engineering, started actual development of the X engine in the "fireplace room" of the old Dearborn tractor plant.

Perhaps Farkas might have progressed faster than he did except, sandwiched in with the X engine development, there was considerable work on both V-6 and straight six engines, undoubtedly at the inisistence of Edsel Ford and Ernest Kanzler. Lawrence Sheldrick, working with Farkas, recalled later that "Mr. Ford would only go so far with the six cylinder engine, and then something would happen to throw cold water on it." However, a few six cylinder, Model T type engines were built; some were even fitted into the Model T chassis for testing. Two of these engines survive in the Henry Ford Museum; one having a small bore and long stroke is compacted into the same length as the regular four cylinder Model T engine and fits into the regular chassis. The other, better designed, is nearly ten inches longer and requires a longer chassis.

But Mr. Ford frowned on lengthening his Model T chassis, believing it not quite adequate for the increased weight and increased power of the straight six engine. Then, too, he never forgot his unsatisfactory six of 1906, Model K (SEE FIG. 17). Henry Ford did not favor the conventional "six" any more than Edsel Ford favored the radical "X-8"; consequently, father and son were actually working at cross purposes much of the time.

But, right or wrong, Henry Ford was the boss so the six cylinder engine work was soon completely submerged to a stepped-up program for producing the X-8 engine. By April of 1925, Farkas finally had an air-cooled prototype ready for testing.

This X-8 engine, pictured in Fig. 19, was indeed compact and extremely unusual looking with its two flywheel fans at either end for cooling the cylinders. Later attempts to use these for supercharging the carburetor failed because of their relatively low speed. The finned cylinders were cast in pairs with integral heads and with the "L" type valve arrangement so dear to the heart of Henry Ford because of its simplicity. As a complete change from Model T, the ignition was by high tension spark coil and battery, and the generator and starter were combined in one unit. Unusual, too, was the use of anti-friction roller bearings for the crankshaft. Bore and stroke were 3⅜" x 4", giving the engine a total displacement of 286 cubic inches—more than one and one half times that of Model T.

The pistons were another of Henry Ford's innovations—all steel! He had quit using any aluminum in his cars since 1916 because he could not arrange quantity buying at a more favorable price with the "aluminum monopoly." Therefore, in order to obtain light-weight pistons, he began a long period of development of thin steel pistons to replace the heavy cast iron pistons then common in the industry. These steel pistons were finally perfected but never used in Model T—nor yet in MODEL A, which Henry Ford at last allowed to be fitted with aluminum pistons.

When the time came for road testing the X engine, it proved to be entirely too heavy for the Model T chassis. Sheldrick, in his reminiscences, recalled having then bought a used Oldsmoboile and fitting the X engine —with, of course, a planetary transmission—into it. "120" was the number for that experimental car and trouble was its name.

Its road tests were far from satisfactory; the lower cylinders fouled inside with lubricating oil and outside with dirt and water thrown up by the front wheels. Furthermore, in order to obtain sufficient road clearance for the lower cylinders, the engine had to be mounted with the crankshaft high in the frame. This brought the drive-shaft well above the normal floor level which was already nearly two feet above the ground. The abominable drive-shaft tunnel was as yet unknown to the industry.

However, the X engine project was continued with hope, but amid a confusion of variations and divided responsibilities, by Ford Engineering until late in 1926 when Henry Ford at last ordered the work stopped. All that remains today of the radical X car are eight engines of varying design—some air cooled, some water cooled—stored in the old Jute Mill in the Greenfield Village at Dearborn.

Surely part of Henry Ford's reluctance to abandon Model T in 1926 was due to the fact that its planned successor, his pet X car, was not yet perfected. Model T's actual successor fell far short of his ideal, but time had already run out for his personal creation. Thus it was that Henry Ford at last yielded, almost too late, to Edsel's program for a more practical, more popular type of car—a program which brought forth the MODEL A. This was Edsel's day and, in many respects, this was Edsel's car. Henry Ford's X car was dead; it remained unknown.

But the elder Ford's day was to come again—December 7, 1931. Then it was that his revolutionary "en bloc" V-8 engine—perhaps the metamorphosis of his X-8—made its dramatic appearance in the restyled 1932 Ford car. *This* engine was Henry Ford's greatest automotive creation, his last mechanical triumph!

Again he was twenty years ahead of the industry. Had Mr. Ford's lifetime been extended only five more years he would have seen every other American manufacturer finally follow his lead by producing en bloc V-8 engines for *their* cars, too.

Photo courtesy Research and Information Dept., Ford Motor Company.

FIGURE 20. "FAREWELL, MY LOVELY!"

On Thursday, May 26, 1927, came the official end for the "Universal Car" with the assembling of the 15,000,000th Model T, although last-minute orders from die-hard motorists forced the building of some 400,000 more of these Tin Lizzies.

At 10 A.M. the engine was completed in the Rouge plant and, with an appropriately simple ceremony, each digit of its serial number was stamped on the block by one of the eight oldest employees in proper order: John F. Wandersee, August Degener, Frank Kulick, Fred L. Rockelman, P. E. Martin, C. B. Hartner, Charles E. Sorensen, and Charles Meida.

The engine was then taken to the Highland Park plant where Henry and Edsel Ford followed it along the chassis and body assembly line until, about 3 P.M., the finished Touring car emerged, inscribed in silver letters, "The Fifteen Millionth Ford." Then Henry Ford, with Edsel driving, made the 14-mile trip back to the Dearborn Engineering Laboratory for another simple ceremony involving his 1896 quadricycle and his first 1909 Model T.

The end of that day found Henry Ford tired but happy, as observed by his engineer, Gene Farkas, who recalls: "He streched himself. He usually made some exercise with his arm when he was tired. He said 'Now, Gene, we've got to do it,' meaning that we've got to design a new car in a hurry."*

All three of the cars mentioned here are preserved together in a special Henry Ford exhibit in the Henry Ford Museum, Dearborn, Michigan.

*This account appears in "FORD, Expansion and Challenge" by Allan Nevins and Frank Ernest Hill.

CHAPTER IV
DECIMATION AND DECISION

While MODEL A itself appeared almost overnight, the decision for it came painfuly slow and at great cost.

For a period of several years before 1928, many a key man in the Ford organization, wittingly or not, had sacrificed his job in paving the way for Model T's successor. While Henry Ford encouraged originality in thinking and welcomed progress in production equipment and production methods, and would readily scrap expensive machine tools for improved ones, he stubbornly resisted any change in Model T itself. He jealously guarded every one of its antiquated features—the planetary transmission, the inadequate brakes, the primitive ignition system, the outmoded bodies. Model T was his—he would allow no one to criticize it—much less touch it.

Those who presumed to mention Model T's shortcomings, those who expressed concern for product progress and improvement were looked upon with suspicion and branded "faithless" by Henry Ford, who then proceeded to "weed them out" of the company by devious means. Usually Harry Bennett or Charles Sorensen did this weeding out for him. Not even his own son, Edsel, escaped this suspicion on occasions, although Henry Ford then often sought out someone else to blame for "influencing Edsel."

Relations between Henry Ford and Edsel Ford once reached such a state that the elder Ford ordered Sorenson to send Edsel—the company president—out to their California branch and to keep him there until ordered to come back. However, Sorensen knew that Edsel would not acept such an order from him, so delayed the message long enough for Henry Ford to cool off and for good feeling to return.

It was this struggle over policy between father and son that was the chief reason for the delay in bringing out MODEL A. Many knowledgeable persons in the Ford Motor Company believed, therefore, that Model T was continued at least two years too long and that the MODEL A appeared two years too late.

Model T had lost its appeal in spite of its low price; the Ford sales executives were unhappy about Model T's obsolescense and the customers and dealers were complaining bitterly about it. Henry Ford knew this but refused to believe it. "All this," he said, "proves just one fact: the company has departed from its fundamental principles and lost its original verve." Dogmatically he told his sales organization, "Most of your trouble at the present time is a question of your mental attitude. The Ford car is a tried and proved product that requires no tinkering. It has met all the conditions of transportation the world over. Changes in style from time to time are merely evolution.

"We do not intend to make a 'six,' an 'eight,' or anything else outside of our regular products. It is true that we have experiments with such cars, as we have experiments with many things. They keep our engineers busy—prevent them from tinkering too much with the Ford car."

That line of reasoning, according to Sorensen, at that particular time only increased the impatience of Edsel and his friends. And most valuable of Edsel's friends was Ernest C. Kanzler, his brother-in-law.

Kanzler was a young lawyer with no industrial experience when brought into the Ford organization in 1919. He served first as an assistant to Sorensen under whom he obtained a good knowledge of all aspects of the business. Edsel Ford soon made him Second Vice President administering production, and influencing sales and advertising policy. But his closeness to Edsel and his proved executive ability aroused only jealousy in Henry Ford, who accused him of influencing Edsel. Mr. Ford made his feeling about Kanzler known to Sorensen in his observation, "That young fellow is getting too big for his breeches."

Ernest Kanzler certainly knew the fate of other high-ranking officials who had spoken openly for improvements to Model T; perhaps he also knew of the near-banishment of even Edsel for pressing his father for an improved car. At any rate, Kanzler, then only 34, knowingly jeopardized his bright future in the Ford Motor Company by presenting a well-argumented plea for a new Ford car in an unsigned memorandum to Henry Ford on January 26, 1926.

In it he alone dared to express the facts, feelings, and beliefs which were shared—but not openly—by such other executives as Rockleman, Sorensen, Martin, Sheldrick, Wills, Galamb, Ryan, and Farkas. This keenly analytical memorandum, now on file in the Ford Motor Company archives, is quoted almost in full because it presents the clearest picture of Henry Ford's personal power but declining position in the industry at the time.

It is indeed conceivable that Ernest Kanzler's plea may actually have directed Henry Ford's thinking, in spite of himself, toward an improved car.

The memorandum is eloquent:

1-26-26

This memorandum is given you so that I can feel that I have dealt honestly and squarely with the responsibility you have given me. It hurts me to write it because I am afraid it may change your feeling for me, and that you may think me unsympathetic and lacking in confidence in your future plans.

Please, Mr. Ford, understand that I realize fully that you have built up this whole business, that it has been your battle and your creation and that all of the Company's successes day after day regardless by whom personally conducted are nevertheless a direct result of your conception and will really be your personal accomplishment for many years even after your lifetime . . .

From the things you have said you above all others recognize the need for:

(A) An intermediate car
(B) Greater power, smoothness, refinement of the Model T type of car
(C) Something for European requirements

1. If we face the facts we must know there is little chance for the production of a tried and thoroughly tested X type car within eighteen months which would not be before the summer of 1927.

Those of us who have been privileged to follow the X development look into the future and hope for great things, BUT, and this is what worries me, I feel that there should also be other developments in process on a power unit along conventional lines so that we would have if necessary a power unit to maintain our position in the automobile field until the X motor is perfected—something which will serve until you will have been given a fair chance to produce the X motors to their final stages of development so that when once adopted they will lead all others for another twenty years like the Model T.

Such a motor can be installed in the intermediate chassis and hold this market for us against competition until such time as we would sweep all before us with your revolutionary X power plant substituted when its perfection has been achieved.

2. While there is every logical engineering argument in favor of the X type, yet we have all our eggs in one basket. It might take much longer than expected to get it perfected and until it should perform greatly better that the present conventional sixes the public will hardly welcome the change.

3. I know of no one who feels more deeply than you the obligation to the 180 odd thousand employees who have started to make their life-work with the company.

4. I think there will always be a field for 4,000 to 5,000 Model T's per day, but I do not think the Model T will continue to be a satisfactory product to maintain our position in the automobile field until the X models have been developed.

We have made over 100 million dollars the last two years each and will probably make 100 million next year, BUT

We have not gone ahead in the last few years, have barely held our own, whereas competition has made great strides. You have always said you either go forward or backwards, you can't stand still.

5. In the past twelve months the other manufacturers have gained tremendously. Our production and sales in 1925 were less than in 1924.

Our Ford customers, particularly the two- and four-door customers, are going to other manufacturers, and our best dealers are low in morale and not making the money they used to.

In spite of the higher prices, the public is choosing six-cylinder cars. In 1924 fourteen makers sold 30% as many sixes as we sold Fords. In 1925 these same makers sold 54% as many six-cylinders cars as we sold Fords—and each one of these fourteen increased his sales, some 400%.

6. There may be theoretical engineering objections to a six, but in every one I have ever driven there has been a most satisfactory smoothness and power range entirely different from and far superior to 4-cylinder performance and almost as good as the Lincoln. This is not only my view, but also that of the public as demonstrated by the way they have opened their pocketbooks to buy sixes.

Practically every man in your organization to whom you have entrusted the greatest responsibility holds the same opinion . . .

9. Could we not carry out your ideas that the product must be made right as expressed in your page of January 16th, 1926 DEARBORN INDEPENDENT. Won't you permit the organization to develop a refined 6-cylinder motor without imposing in any way on the time of those working on the X motors. Such a power plant would never be used unless its performance satisfies you that it has real merit . . .

The advantage of this memorandum is that I can write certain things that I find it difficult to say to you. It is one of the handicaps of the power of your personality which you perhaps least of all realize, but most people, when with you, hesitate to say what they think.

13. It is unique in the commercial history of the world that one man should run away with the field as you have done in the motor industry. We have had a wonderful head start because your first designs of a car were 20 years ahead of the world, as well as your methods of production and marketing.

But we are losing our position because the world has learned from you and with its combined efforts, each learning from the other, it has now devloped a product that is alarmingly absorbing the public's purchasing power.

14. The best evidence that conditions are not right is in the fact that with most of the bigger men in the organization there is a growing uneasiness because things are not right—they feel our position weakening and our grip slipping. We are no longer sure that when we plan increased facilities that they will be used. The buoyant spirit of confident expansion is lacking. And we know we have been defeated and licked in England. And we are being caught up in the United States. With every additional car our competitors sell they get stronger and we get weaker.

Even on the basis of equal design value we could still out-distance all competition because of our "from mine to finished car" ability to produce, and unified ownership. But with our competitors' volume increasing they are rapidly approaching our formerly unique powers of producing at lowered cost. Inwardly we are alarmed to see our advantage ebbing away, knowing that the counter-measures to prevent it are not immediately at hand. We all realize that an epoch making motor such as we expect the X lines to be cannot be the product of the immediate future.

This feeling exists not outwardly, but I will stake my reputation it exists in every important man in the Company. I, personally, have helped to stamp this feeling down wherever it has tried to break through.

The writing of this has not been pleasing, Mr. Ford, but I have always tried to tell you what I see and feel.

These thoughts have been uppermost in my mind the last year and I cannot keep from expressing them any longer.

Sincerely,

There was no known reply to Kanzler's memorandum, but Henry Ford thereafter treated him with studied rudeness and even ridicule so that, exactly six months later, Kanzler left the Ford Motor Company—but not the Ford sphere. He joined the Guardian Trust group, in Detroit, and headed the new Universal Credit Corporation formed to handle the financing of MODEL A for the dealers, and for the flood of new customers.

Following Kanzler's removal came many more, reaching from high in the executive level well down into the foreman level. Avery, Hartner, and Findlater with dozens of other capable men had left, and William Ryan, the only man who both Henry and Edsel Ford agreed was the "perfect sales manager," left soon after. Sorensen, having taken his cue from Henry Ford, had started his far reaching purge of those whom he called "the Model T men" from the Highland Park plant. In vain did William Klann, then a forceful figure in Ford production, protest these firings. But Sorensen and Bennett ruled the company organization, with the nod from Henry Ford; and soon Bill Klann himself was gone.

To most observers, the colossal change-over from Model T to MODEL A appeared to be an almost impossible task for the time available; and the coincidental decimation of the very men most needed to effect the change-over seemed to be nothing short of industrial suicide.

But somehow Henry Ford's usual but unorthodox method of ignoring "experts" and of assigning inexperienced men to key posts again paid off with the amazing production record of MODEL A.

"By any standards of measurement," wrote the historian, Alan Nevins, "this rebirth of the Ford automobile must be accounted one of the most striking achievements of twentieth century industrial history. Though Henry Ford's stubborn delay in recognizing the necessity of change had made the human and monetary costs greater than they need have been, they were lower than most observers had anticipated."

We have already noted something of the human costs to Ford; what were the monetary costs? Henry Ford was never sure. "All I know," he said, "is that when we started actually to work out this change of models we had $350,000,000 in the bank. Now we have worked it out and we have $250,000,000 in the bank. That means we have spent $100,000,000 in the operation."

A more careful examination of the operation indicated the costs to be closer to $250,000,000 including retooling costs and loss of profits during the change-over period. Such was the price paid by Henry Ford for his delayed decision.

Photo courtesy Research and Information Dept., Ford Motor Company.

FIGURE 21. MODEL A — A NEW ERA.

Edsel's MODEL A Roadster, 40-A, photographed May 28, 1928, at the Ford Engineering Laboratory, shows the decided improvement in proportions and appearance over Model T.

Notice how the exposed fuel tank sets on top of the side panels and itself forms a graceful part of the cowl. The new all-steel bodies were made possible by special jigs and welding techniques developed by Ford for MODEL A. Even at this date, outside door handles had not yet appeared on the open cars. With Model A, Henry Ford began buying tires from manufacturers other than Firestone alone; this car is fitted with the Goodyear "Diamond Tread."

Body colors in 1928 were gunmetal blue, Niagara blue (more like olive green), dawn gray, and Arabian sand; all wheels, fenders, and running gear were black. All brightwork was nickel plated; upholstering was brown grained imitation leather; tops were black grained Fabricoid; steering wheels were red plastic.

Photo by Kenneth Stauffer, AACA Photographer.

FIGURE 22. ANOTHER FORD "FIRST" — 1929 STATION WAGON.

Owned and partially restored by Joseph Strickland West Chester, Pa.

Ford pioneered the assembly line production of Station Wagons in the industry with this model in 1929—all other station wagons were more or less "custom built" and fitted to "commercial chassis" in the plants of several independent body builders.

This is one of the less than 5,000 "genuine" 150-A Ford Station Wagons in 1929 and is factory-assembled with a Murray body. All these were produced in *only one color combination*—natural wood finish, black fenders and wheels, Manilla brown cowl, hood, and coupe pillar. There is a full seat front and rear with two folding seats in the center; rear seat is removable. *(See also Figs. 9, 23 and 33.)*

Photo by Bill Hall.

FIGURE 23. A "GENUINE" 1929 FORD STATION WAGON — CURTAINS UP!

Owned and restored by William Hall, Zanesville, Ohio.

Another of the rare "factory assembled" 150-A Station Wagons, this MODEL A is numbered A1684848 and has a Murray body, number M250-3203. *(See also Fig. 22.)*

Bill Hall, president of the Model "A" Restorers' Club, acquired the car from a Vermont school for girls and restored it to like-new condition. It won first prize in the annual Hartford, Conn. AUTORAMA.

This view shows the *original* side curtains in place and illustrates the cut-out door for clearing the side-mounted spare wheel.

CHAPTER V
NEW CREATION

MODEL A was born of necessity, a child of adversity. It was forced upon Henry Ford who was not mentally "set" for it and whose organization was not physically prepared for it. But fortunately, the past was prologue for MODEL A; it was the undeliberated sum of all that had gone before it in the Ford Motor Company. And, being distinctly "Ford" in background and features, it was patently the kind of car that could have been built nowhere else successfully. Not the result of long and directed planning—Ford Engineering was not then set up to operate on long-range projects—MODEL A actually sprang into being in less than a year through the integration and compromise of the latent ideas of Edsel Ford, Henry Ford, and the many engineers steeped in the Ford way.

Once Henry Ford had made his decision for MODEL A, the work of its creation went forward at a furious but often interrupted pace. There was naturally a great deal of confusion in the Ford Motor Company, and in the Ford Engineering Department in particular, when Henry Ford suddenly ordered work started on an entirely new car. This condition was not lessened any by the continued decimation of Ford personnel. Then, too, Henry Ford was making so many assignments, reassignments, and divisions of authority within the Company that progress in designing MODEL A was further hampered. Only he knew from day to day just what was being accomplished with the new car—or perchance, even *he* knew not!

Though the new car was at first neither Henry Ford's idea nor ideal he was quick to adopt it as *his* MODEL A Ford. Certainly it was never entirely *his*, as was Model T, for while he actually "approved" most of MODEL A he had "dictated" all of Model T. Thus, for Henry Ford, the designing of MODEL A was a combination of his approvals, dictates, rejections, concessions, and compromises.

There were many excellent Ford engineers working on MODEL A who had well formulated ideas for the new car, but none was entirely free to develop his ideas alone. Everything about MODEL A had to be cleared through its chief engineer, Lawrence Sheldrick, for Henry Ford's approval. While this method probably forestalled chaos and kept Mr. Ford informed of every little detail, it also served to slow things down just when speed was most needed. Henry Ford could have delegated *some* of the detail work to advantage.

But with all the delays, MODEL A was created with remarkable speed—so fast, in fact, that many of its parts went directly from the drawing board into production and, in the latter stages of its birth, some of the plant layout and some of the new special machine tools were designed simultaneously with the specific parts of the car each was to accommodate.

Since the prolonged period for decision had extended almost to the end of 1926 it left no time in 1927 for extensive experimenting, thorough developing, or exhaustive testing such as usually attends the birth of a completely new and successful car. MODEL A had to be exactly *right* the first time—and it was!

The need for a new transmission in any new Ford car was basic and this issue was forced by Edsel Ford months before Henry Ford ever conceded to a successor of any kind for Model T. That a new transmission was the first of Henry Ford's many, many compromises between *his* ideal car and the final product, MODEL A, is well attested by Henry Ford's closest associate, Charles E. Sorensen. As chief of Ford production as well as Mr. Ford's right-hand man, Sorensen was "in" on the designing of MODEL A right from the start. He wrote in his book, MY FORTY YEARS WITH FORD:

"With the coming of MODEL A, Edsel became more of a factor in policy matters. He was willing to step out on his own. He now wanted MODEL A to meet the popular features of competitors' cars. He wanted a shifting gear transmission, and there was more trouble with his father on that.

"The Model T planetary was the elder Ford's idea for the future car. He called the shifting gear a 'crunch gear.' He said the transmission would never stand up because the gears would clash when changing speeds." (This was a paradoxical statement for Henry Ford who was, even then, building the Lincoln car with a sliding gear transmission which stood up very well!—Author's note.)

Sorensen further stated: "Mr. Ford discussed an *automatic planetary transmission* with me. I realized there would be a lot of development work to do before that could be ready for production. MODEL A's sliding gear transmission was the result of a compromise between Edsel and his father.

"There was never any real acceptance of this by Henry Ford. As he put it, 'We are imitating others.' Although he could not see how to make his planetary transmission automatic then, look where it is today. Hydramatic transmissions are the planetary type with automatic clutches actuated by hydraulic pressure.

"Had Mr. Ford understood a torque converter that is used in transmissions today, I am sure he would have had his way on the MODEL A transmission. It would *not* have been a sliding gear type."

Lawrence Sheldrick recalled that "in 1926 Mr. Ford finally conceded to some type of sliding gear transmission on which I worked until commissioned to start designs for a new four cylinder engine of larger displacement than Model T." Then Frank Johnson, of the Lincoln group, was assigned to the transmission design which, with a multiple disc, dry clutch, was to be a miniature counterpart of the Lincoln. Henry Ford thought it wasteful of power to have the countershaft, or cluster gears, turning idly all the time the car would be running in "high gear" which is a direct drive. But no practical way could be found to disengage these gears when not needed. The Warner gear people were called upon for help for MODEL A's transmission, but the final product was actually a miniature of the Lincoln design.

Sheldrick was assigned to engine design late in 1926 and, as stated in his reminiscences, "we followed the Model T only in the respect that it was to be a four cylinder, L head engine of the same general type but with a number of improvements. Specifications 'just grew' from this start." For example, the new crankshaft was the same length as in Model T but was made much stronger and had larger journals.

It was characteristic of Henry Ford that he should concentrate on an improved power plant for the new car, and he took a personal interest in the engine work. According to Sheldrick, "Mr. Ford wanted full-size sketches of the engine, vertically, in front of him. We used a cloth 'blackboard,' which could be rolled up, and different colored chalk for drawing the various parts. He found the usual intricate drawings with sections and views, one upon the other, a little difficult to follow."

Harold Hicks, who had earlier distinguished himself by work on the World War I "Liberty" aircraft engines, played a very important part in the engine development for MODEL A. In a recent interview, Hicks recalled that he was brought in on the engine project in April, 1927. "I was called down to the north end of the big room at the dynamometer section (of the Ford Engineering Laboratory). There were Sorensen, Martin, and Edsel Ford. They showed me an engine that was running on the block. Sorensen said, 'Well, Hicks, we've got here an engine which is 203 cubic inches (Model T was 176) but it is only developing 22 horsepower (Model T was 20). If we should give you charge of this development, how much could you increase it?'

"I took my slide rule, did a few calculations, and said, 'I think I can get you 40 horsepower'."

Hicks was given the job. He asked for two months in which to complete the work, but Sorensen gave him only one month.

Hicks continued, "With Carl Schultz to draw up a manifold, we got out first a Y type manifold in only seven days, using certain principles I had obtained from Colonel Hall 'way back on the World War I "Liberty" engines. This gave 30 horsepower right off."

But there was more to do! He found there were insufficient water passages around the exhaust valve ports and had them opened up. He and Edsel Ford both believed the valves themselves were too small in diameter, so these were enlarged and the horsepower went up to 34. Hicks realized that the original vaporizer type manifold and carburetor designed by Holley did not give sufficient speed range for a 40 horsepower engine of that size. Therefore he went to his friend, Howard Manwaring, in the Zenith Carburetor Company for a test carburetor. And then, only three weeks after he had started his job, Hicks had the engine developing the promised 40 horsepower!

Hicks wanted other improvements in the engine; he tried to have the crankshaft journals all increased to 1¾" (Model T bearings were only 1¼"). But, according to Hicks, Edsel came to him later on and told him, "Father does not agree with you that the journals should be larger in diameter. He feels that they should be small so that the crankshaft will be limber enough to follow the bearings in the crankcase." So MODEL A kept its original 1⅜" main bearings and its 1½" rod bearings.

Henry Ford was at that time supposedly laid up at Fair Lane recovering from an automobile accident. This not only served to keep him out of court as defendant in the Sapiro libel suit against his DEARBORN INDEPENDENT newspaper for the anti-semitic articles which had appeared therein, but this also kept him from witnessing the engine test and from seeing the Zenith carburetor on the job.

Joe Galamb, another of MODEL A's creators, added this sidelight on the matter of the carburetor, "Holley had a terrific 'in' at Ford Motor Company as a bosom friend of Henry Ford. Hicks knew this and cleverly needled Sorensen each time he came down to watch dynamometer tests by saying, 'Of course, we are developing 40 horsepower, but you'll never use the Zenith carburetor.' Finally Sorensen said, 'Why in hell do you keep telling me we won't use the Zenith carburetor? By God, we are going to! You get the Zenith Company in!'"

Because of Sorensen, Henry Ford accepted the Zenith carburetor, but not without first giving it his personal touch. Hicks continued, "I remember they had too many bolts holding it together—Henry Ford said to me, 'cut those bolts down.' I had Zenith get out a new design ... and I felt quite proud that they had reduced the number of bolts from fourteen to two. Mr. Ford looked at it and said, 'Two is too many. Make just one bolt!' So the MODEL A carburetor came out with just a single bolt down through it." Hicks' choice of carburetor was vindicated in a final test he ran for Henry Ford on July 28, 1927 with the carburetors of Holley, Stromberg, and Kingston all competing unsuccessfully with Zenith.

Hicks' original Y type manifold never went into production because he "had to put a certain amount of heat on the job to make it manifold correctly." His final manifold was more successful because of the heat operation.

The characteristic MODEL A tapered muffler welded into a single unit with exhaust and tail pipe was Hicks' design to which Henry Ford added his own personal touch in the form of a "V" shaped *forged* clamp to hold the exhaust pipe to the manifold. About this Harold Hicks said, "At this time, throughout the MODEL A development, Henry Ford went forging crazy—everything had to be a forging—even on the carburetors there were little forgings for controlling the throttle and choke valves."

Even "Sheet Metal Joe" Galamb, as he was affectionately called by Henry Ford, complained about the indiscriminate use of forgings for the brackets to support fenders, lamps, and running boards. He knew those brackets could be made just as strong but much cheaper with pressed sheet metal. It took Galamb nearly a year to demonstrate to Mr. Ford that he could have strong steel brackets and save $30 in the cost of MODEL A. Late in 1928 Fords began to lose some of their expensive forgings; by early 1929 pressed steel had pretty well taken over the body brackets.

But Henry Ford's insistence then on many forgings was based on two things: he had just put a large forging shop in operation and, to him, forgings had always meant "quality." Here was his chance to put his new shop to work and to put quality into his new car at the same time! He counted not the high cost of forgings—then.

Henry Ford contributed other of his own ideas to the MODEL A engine design which, however, often added to expense in time, money, and difficulty of manufacture. His insistence on a "mushroom" foot on the engine valve stems, for instance, was good from the standpoint of reducing stem end wear and thus enabled the Ford valves to last the life of the engine without adjustment. (No provision was ever made for "adjusting" valves in any Ford engine until the overhead valve engine was built in recent years.) The "mushroom" valves were more expensive and more difficult to manufacture than conventional valves and in addition required expensive split guide bushings in order to be assembled in the engine.

Lawrence Sheldrick recalled also that, "the original crankshaft had thick discs or 'cheeks' between the throws, a machining extravagance which Mr. Ford explained he wanted because some time he wanted to put

30

on counterweights and then every car in the field could have them added. These 'cheeks' were actually ground to close tolerances. Later they were eliminated."

Other of Henry Ford's peculiar ideas involved the connecting rods. At first he wanted forged "X" section rods, then welded tubular section rods in the early MODEL A engines. But neither of these was as satisfactory as the conventional "I" section rods which he soon had to approve for all subsequent production. Some few MODEL A engines may still be running with these unusual connecting rods in them. About the fitting of MODEL A connecting rods, Lawrence Sheldrick had this to say, "Mr. Ford insisted, contrary to all engineering principles, that there be no clearance between the connecting rods and the piston pin bosses. This caused what appeared to be piston slap but was really rod slap between the pin bosses. This practice was discontinued within the first year of production," and a clearance of .040" to .053" was maintained thereafter.

Hating to purchase patented units for his new car, Henry Ford always attempted to design his own. Often he was spectacularly successful in such ventures, sometimes not. The Ford designed "Abell" electric starter was one such failure; it frequently jammed on the flywheel ring gear, chewed up teeth, remained engaged with the engine running, and bent the ½" drive shaft. Mr. Ford was forced to go to the Bendix people for a successful electric starter for MODEL A. Characteristically, the new Bendix starter (with a ⅝" shaft, incidentally) was designed so that it could be fitted in place of the unsuccessful Abell starters as they failed in the field. Henry Ford rarely made an improvement that couldn't easily be adapted to cars already in the hands of his customers.

Of course, many of Henry Ford's peculiar ideas were very good. One of these was his single control for choking and adjusting the carburetor from the dash panel. No other automobile had such a convenient manual control, if any at all, for adjusting for smooth warm-up or economical fuel consumption.

Another of his good ideas was that of forging the rear axle and differential gear in one piece. This unit was not only stronger but six machining operations were eliminated along with the labor of assembling the gear, key, and two lock rings on a separate shaft, as in Model T. Such ideas became practical with the advent of new alloy steels and Henry Ford's new forging plant.

Harold Hicks indirectly made one more contribution to the MODEL A—because of an automobile accident! He was road testing one of the experimental cars when an old truck pulled right out in front of him. In the resulting crash, Hicks and a passenger were thrown through the windshield and were badly injured and severely cut. Henry Ford and Edsel both looked at the wreck and decided then and there to put laminated "safety glass" in the windshield of MODEL A. This was another Ford "first," as was their method of making the glass in a continuous strip rather than in small batches.

The accident and the subsequent hospitalization ended Hicks' work with MODEL A. When he at last recovered he was returned to duty as Chief Airplane Engineer of the Stout Metal Airplane Division of the Ford Motor Company. Henry Ford's activities in the pioneering of mass production of all-metal airplanes just prior to and during this expansive period of the MODEL A car are worth noting here:

Back in 1924 Henry Ford had bought up the Stout Metal Airplane Company which proposed to build a new kind of airplane which was still to be designed. Henry Ford became extremely enthusiastic at first but came to lose faith in William B. Stout as a designer only after having given much publicity to him and to the new airplane he was to build with Ford. This may have been unjust to Stout who was actually a good automotive and aircraft designer with radical and advanced ideas. But, believing he had bought a "lemon" in the airplane company and not wanting the world to know it, Henry Ford directed Harold Hicks, in January of 1926, to "get in there and build that airplane and keep Stout out of there." Hicks did the job, Stout got the credit, and Henry Ford "saved face." The famous Ford Tri-Motor airplane was a tremendous success and proved to be as rugged and as durable as the MODEL A car. Ford Tri-Motors are still flying in regular service!

To accommodate the manufacture of the airplanes, Henry Ford began in 1924 to build his airport between Southfield Road and Oakwood Boulevard in Dearborn. Then, in 1928, on a two-hundred acre plot just north of the airport, he began construction of the Henry Ford Museum (SEE FIG. 30), the Greenfield Village of historic buildings, and his unique school system. All these comprise the Edison Institute named in honor of, and dedicated by his esteemed friend, Thomas A. Edison (SEE FIG. 28). President Hoover took part in the dedication on October 21, 1929. The Greenfield Village today plays host to annual gatherings, called "meets," of antique automobiles of all types and ages as well as MODEL A Fords. (SEE FIGS. 41 AND 71).

To complete this area, the beautiful Dearborn Inn was opened in 1931 on Oakwood Boulevard as the world's first "airport hotel." It is still the center of attraction for Dearborn visitors although the airport activities have been discontinued since 1937. The airfield is now used as the one of the proving grounds by the Ford Motor Company.

These projects were but a few of the many other interests absorbing much of Henry Ford's time and energy during this important period of the Ford Motor Company. Henry Ford continued to invade many new fields even while struggling to maintain his leadership in the automotive field.

Of course, Henry Ford had many able lieutenants working to recapture the Ford share of the automobile market with development of MODEL A. Not the least of these was his own son. Edsel originated and carried out the style design of the MODEL A body, and when Jimmy Hughes left Ford for Studebaker, Joe Galamb was brought into the body work. An entirely new concept of body building was evolved. For the first time in automotive history bodies were not only built without a wooden framework, but they were temporarily held together by specially designed jigs while all the seams wer electrically welded by machines to form a unit body. Engineer Bredo Berghoff called this electric welding of the car "the outstanding feature of the MODEL A tool-up."

As MODEL A's chief engineer, Sheldrick pointed out, "Messrs. Martin and Sorensen influenced the design of the car as a whole, as well as did Mr. Ford, as far as making things suitable for economical production." While Mr. Ford's actions did not indicate he was always as "economy minded" as Sheldrick mentions, this coordination between design and production was extremely

Photo courtesy Research and Information Dept., Ford Motor Company.

FIGURE 24. THE RIVER ROUGE PLANT — HEART OF FORD'S EMPIRE.

Looking north at the Ford Motor Company's 1,115-acre plant on the River Rouge we can see first the open hearth building, the rolling mill, and the pressed steel and the spring and upset building on the left. In the center are the ore ship basin and storage bins; north of the basin are the glass plant, cement plant, paper mill, small power house, and the large "B" building; to the right are the blast furnaces, foundry, and motor assembly plant. The battery of eight tall stacks on the right is part of the spotless Ford power plant facing Miller Road.

The northern boundary road (now called Rotunda Drive) leads off to the left to the Ford Airport (now the proving ground) and the Henry Ford Museum and Greenfield Village.

Ford's own railroad, ships and trucks brought raw materials from Ford's own forests, mines and farms to the Rouge plant where they were processed and fabricated into finished Ford cars.

Photo courtesy The Henry Ford Museum.

FIGURE 25. MODEL A HOMECOMING!

Each year the Henry Ford Museum plays host to MODEL A owners in the Model A Restorers' Club. Here are more than 100 of these fabulous cars assembled at a MARC meet near the "Ann Arbor House" in the Greenfield Village, Dearborn, Michigan. (See also Fig. 84).

important, for many new machine tools had to be designed and built. And the new tools had to operate at higher speeds and on tougher alloys than those for old Model T.

With all his other absorbing projects and interests, Henry Ford not only found time to review the results and direct the work of his lieutenants, but he continued to inject many of his own ideas, some of which gave MODEL A its unique characteristics, and some of which added to its cost in time or money.

The cowl-mounted gravity fuel tank, while not Henry Ford's original idea, was his adopted ideal; it was extremely simple and simplicity appealed to him. His first lay-out for the tank was dated January 20, 1926, and was intended for the last of the Model T. cars. Furthermore, Henry Ford did not like the vacuum tank system and, having no faith in the fuel pumps then on the market, he would have none of these on his new car. It remained only for Edsel, then, to give the tank uniqueness by designing it as an actual and visible part of the cowl of MODEL A.

This fuel tank which Mr. Ford wanted in MODEL A was perfectly all right except for the unreasonably dim view taken of it by a few states. It was thought of as a "safety hazard" because all the fuel was "located right in the laps of the passengers." (At this time Chevrolet was making the most of the situation by advertising their "safety" fuel tank situated under the frame at the back of the car!)

Consequently, Sheldrick had to hold up the design of MODEL A and take time to confer with state officials in Massachusetts, Connecticut and New Jersey before he could get their reluctant approvals of the fuel tank position. Actual tests demonstrated that the Ford fuel tank would not explode even if the gasoline caught fire when filling the tank. The secret of this lay in the little safety screen screwed inside the tank spout which acted the same as the screen on a miner's safety lamp. However, nearly everyone who ever noticed this screen always mistook it for a dirt strainer!

Gene Farkas, who was in charge of developing the suspension, the all-welded wire wheels, the axles, and the new four-wheel brakes, progressed admirably with all but the brakes. And there he was handicapped by some of Ford's ideas that were either illegal or impractical.

Since Henry Ford would have nothing to do with any four-wheel designs already on the market, Farkas had to design a new system that would not be a complicated mechanism nor a patent infringement. His first design included the cam-operated, wedge-adjusted brake shoes linked directly to the foot pedal bar. But Henry Ford demanded an equalizer bar in the linkage. And Farkas, with Sheldrick, the chief engineer, had to take time to install an equalizer bar in a test chassis and demonstrate to Mr. Ford that it made the car skid. They were then allowed to go back to the solid cross-shaft system.

An uncomplicated brake mechanism meant, to Henry Ford, one with a simple linkage of the hand brake lever to "pick up" and "set" the rear brake shoes for parking. All the early MODEL A Fords with the hand lever on the left side had this system. But shortly after the cars appeared on the market, the District of Columbia and Pennsylvania both banned these brakes and forced the redesigning of MODEL A to include a separate set of "emergency" or parking brakes. Gene Farkas then had to redesign the hubs and drums, install a separate pair of brake bands, change the wire wheels, and relocate the hand brake lever from the side to a central position in front of the gear shift lever.

Farkas had an easier time with his other assignments. His first job was to improve the suspension for MODEL A. This had to include Henry Ford's two transverse springs mounted *across* the frame rather than the conventional four lateral springs placed *along* the frame. Many people believed that the two transverse springs must necessarily give a "harder" ride than four lateral springs. But Henry Ford believed otherwise so no Ford car since 1908 had any lateral springs until after his death in 1947.

Regardless of what was *believed,* Henry Ford *knew* that transverse suspension made the springs carry their own weight and so relieved the axles of that much unsprung weight. Then lighter axles and bearings could be used to advantage, and lightness with strength was MODEL A's biggest advantage over its competitors.

The new suspension, while a great improvement over that of Model T, did not satisfy Mr. Ford. He may have laughed along with his customers when they joked that "the pasengers were Model T's shock absorbers," but he wanted no such jokes about MODEL A, which was to be a masterpiece of economy with comfort. He asked Gene Farkas to "get the best shock absorber on the market" for the new car, and Farkas chose the same Houdaille double-acting shock absorbers which they were then using on the high-priced Lincoln.

Thus MODEL A came to pioneer expensive hydraulic shock absorbers on a low-priced, "popular" car—all the others soon followed.

Finally came MODEL A's birthday—Friday, October 21, 1927! The day before, Henry Ford had unceremoniously stamped number "A1" on the first engine (SEE FIG. 24) which was installed, that Friday, in a MODEL A Ford Tudor (SEE FIG. 27) which Henry Ford then used personally for testing and inspection before giving his final approval of the new car. Actual production did not begin until November 1, 1927 and continued at a rate of only about 20 cars per day for some time. (Contrast this slow start with the production record established on June 26, 1929—-9100 Ford cars and trucks built in one day!). But Henry Ford knew that haste then might be fatal; he needed time to train his men carefully in the use of the new machine tools and in the new methods and in the new standards required for building MODEL A. The entire reputation of MODEL A depended upon excellent quality control right from the start.

Although Harold Hicks' injuries had taken him away from the MODEL A work during the last days of its creation, he kept in close contact with it through Henry Ford and others. Hicks recounted later, "The new MODEL A pleased Henry Ford very much. He told me, 'Well, you go out and drive a MODEL A wide open. The other fellows will stick with you for a while. Pretty soon they get tired and then you just go right on ahead of them all!'

"At that time there were few autos that could go above 75 miles an hour; most around 70. The MODEL A was right out there competing with them. Up to 30, the MODEL A could skin the pants off anything that was on the road. Lionel Woolson, Chief Engineer at Packard, called me one day and asked, 'Hicks, what are you fellows out there trying to do? You really have just made us look silly below 30 because we can't catch these MODEL As!'

"It was largely the fact the engine developed high torque, and it was an excellent output at the same time (SEE PAGE 90). The car, because of Mr. Ford's idea of having light weight structure, was not so much mass to move. That is why that car had performance."

That MODEL A had much more than performance to offer, the public was soon to learn. Henry and Edsel Ford and their engineers had created MODEL A of their own eclectic ideas; they used the newest methods, the best materials, and the finest workmanship that could be developed, and Henry Ford had put his final stamp of approval on the new car. Then Henry Ford came to a rather belated realization of Edsel's talents, remarking with real pride, "We've got a pretty good man in my son. He knows style—how a car ought to look. And he has mechanical horse sense, too."

At last the work of creation was done; now was MODEL A ready for presentation to the waiting and excitedly expectant world. No other debutante had ever been prepared with such haste, nor presented with such brilliance, nor received with such enthusiasm as the MODEL A.

Photo courtesy Research and Information Dept., Ford Motor Company.

FIGURE 26. MODEL A IS BORN.

Henry Ford stamped number A1 on the first MODEL A engine off the Rouge plant asembly line Thursday, October 20, 1927. The next day this engine went into a Tudor Sedan *(see Fig. 27)* which Henry Ford used personally for testing and inspection before giving his final approval of the new car. Actual production began November 1 and continued at a rate of only about 20 cars per day while orders for half a million Fords—sight unseen—continued to pile up!

Some time later, Henry Ford ordered this engine installed in a Phaeton (dated 5-31-28) reserved for Edison's use at Dearborn and later used for publicity purposes; the A1 engine now exists, still in the Phaeton, in the Armington & Sims Machine Shop at Greenfield Village.

CHAPTER VI
DEBUT

The second day of December, 1927, dawned sullen and cold; most of the nation was drenched with rain or pelted with sleet or snow. It was indeed a day to drive people indoors, yet actually millions of people were gathered outside FORD showrooms in all our large cities and were clamoring for a first view of the "Debutante of the Century"—MODEL A.

To a people long accustomed to the prosaic Model T, the new Ford was a marvel to behold, and the man who managed to crush as close as ten feet to an enshrined MODEL A considered himself amply rewarded for his long, cold wait, his trampled feet, and his wet and perhaps torn clothing. Such a man was thereby set apart and above his neighbors for he had actually *seen* the MODEL A!

Madison Square Garden, in New York City, was a pandemonium when the new Ford was exhibited there; mounted police were called to keep mobs from crushing through the show windows in Cleveland; Detroit Convention Hall (SEE FIG. 31) was jammed all day as 200,000 people pressed through for a glimpse of the new Fords; 25,000 people turned out in sub-zero weather in St. Paul and 651,000 in Kansas City came out to see MODEL A. And thus it was everywhere, for this was yet a part of the spirit that made up the "roaring twenties."

Not since Armistice Day in 1918 had there been such a tumult in the land. And not even Charles A. Lindbergh's spectacular feat of flying alone across the Atlantic earlier in 1927, was met with greater national ovation than was MODEL A's dramatic appearance that day.

No other automobile, before nor since, ever monopolized the headlines of all city newspapers:

"*Ford's Masterpiece Viewed by Thousands,*" greeted the front page readers of the Brooklyn (N.Y.) *Eagle*, "2,200 see new car in first hour at Brooklyn showroom while police hold back the over-eager. Larger mob storms Ford headquarters on Broadway, Manhattan; 7,000 people seeing the Ford in first hour."

"*No 'Tin Lizzie' Reception,*" the *Eagle* continued, "Soft music ushers in models at dress reception at the Waldorf. This elegance was . . . significant of the Ford's emergence into new realms of glory."

"*200,000 View New Ford Car on First Day,*" reported the New York *American*, "Despite a cold rain, more than 200,000 New Yorkers see new Ford during city exhibition . . . traffic at standstill; police called to keep order! . . . 30,000 orders taken first day; millionaire William Averell Harriman purchases first Ford in city!" (W. Averell Harriman *still* uses a MODEL A on occasions; see Fig. 8—AUTHOR'S NOTE).

"*5,000 See Ford on Friday,*" was the Palm Beach (Fla.) *Post* headline, while the Philadelphia *Inquirer* blazoned, "*New Ford Viewed by 75,000 Persons*" on its front page and continued, "Visitors at first showing include student bodies of public schools . . . spark and throttle levers are sole reminder of the old Model T design!"

These mass demonstrations at the first showings of MODEL A all over the country were but the natural release of six months' build-up of national curiosity and interest, following Ford's news of a new kind of car.

The end of Model T production itself was keenly felt everywhere because of its far-reaching economic and social effects; thousands of Ford dealers had nothing new to sell and some went bankrupt; thousands of Ford employees were idled, along with thousands more who supplied parts, raw materials, transportation, and services to Ford Motor Company and Ford dealers. Naturally, people were interested in the coming of a new Ford car.

National curiosity, lacking official news from Ford, was fed by wild reports and rumors which consistently made newspaper headlines. The whole country wondered and speculated about Ford—"Can Henry Ford come back?"; "Will the new car do as much for America as the Model T"; "Can it be made better than Model T without raising the price too high?"—these questions, and more, were being asked everywhere but nobody had the answers.

Allan Nevins, in *Ford: Expansion and Challenge*, recorded that "scores of millions caught up every rumor: the car was to have a revolutionary new engine; the car was to be called the Edison; the car was to be a hybrid of Lincoln and Ford named Linford; the car was a secret disappointment and Ford was in despair; the car was a dazzling success and would put Chevrolet with the dodo."

"Never in our industrial history," commented B. C. Forbes, "had any product been awaited with half as much tension." And, it might be added, never had any product so fully met all expectations.

Sidney Strong, automobile historian, collector (SEE FIG. 15) and a Director of the AACA, was one of the Ford dealers who made the difficult transition from Model T to MODEL A. His Strong Motor Company in Atwater, Minnesota, is one of the earliest Ford agencies. He recalls the anxious days of waiting for MODEL A, first thirty days delivery was promised, then sixty, and finally ninety—and more—while costs, overhead, and salaries drained finances.

"One day we were called to the assembly plant in St. Paul. We thought then we would see the new Ford but we didn't even see a picture! Instead we were given lists of new equipment, manuals, and an inspiring address by a Ford official. The new Ford, we were told, would be so far advanced that we dealers were just not prepared for it; we must go back and 'put our houses in order.' We would have to set up new parts bins and inventories, and install new and special equipment for 'scientifically' servicing and adjusting the new car.

"I returned home, called a Sunday meeting of all my employees. 'A new age has dawned!' I told them, 'and we must prepare for the MODEL A!' We began a complete face-lifting job on the old showroom and shop; we installed all the new equipment; we studied all the service manuals—and still we waited!

"Finally, MODEL A arrived, and every person in town turned out to see it.

"One of our exhibitions, spectacular at that time, was to race a MODEL A in low gear across the large showroom floor and stop it just short of the plate glass window to demonstrate these wonderful, new four-wheel brakes!"

With the coming of MODEL A, Ford engaged the famous Philadelphia advertising firm, N. W. Ayres, to plan and conduct the publicity for the car. The build-up

35

Photo courtesy Research and Information Dept., Ford Motor Company.

FIGURE 27. FIVE FORDS IN 1928.

Posed with MODEL A Tudor Sedan No. A1 are Edsel Ford, president of the company, and his father, Henry Ford, who founded the company and still owned it.

The two boys are Edsel's sons and future executives of the company, Benson Ford and Henry Ford II. Two other children, Josephine and William, were absent when the photograph was taken.

Photo courtesy Research and Information Dept., Ford Motor Company.

FIGURE 28. HENRY FORD AND THOMAS A. EDISON.

While in the employ of the Detroit Edison Electric Company, Henry Ford was encouraged in the building of his first automobile by his employer, Thomas Edison. Later the two became very close friends and often went on camping jaunts together with Harvey Firestone and John Burroughs, the naturalist.

Just as Henry Ford's employees always called him "Mr. Ford," so he always called his old boss "Mr. Edison." Henry Ford's high esteem of Thomas Edison was evidenced by his naming THE EDISON INSTITUTE (comprising the school, the Henry Ford Museum, and Greenfield Village) in his honor, and by having Thomas Edison dedicate the Henry Ford Museum on October 21, 1939—the fiftieth anniversary of Edison's invention of the first practical incandescent lamp.

of national curiosity was a part of their plan along with well-timed, full-page spreads of advertising copy in all major newspapers and magazines. Ayres convinced Henry Ford on the publicity value inherent in the simultaneous showing of MODEL A throughout the nation. Ford's advertising budget for introducing MODEL A was fantastic—but so were the results!

The biggest problem in arranging the simultaneous showing was lack of Fords to show. There were scarcely five hundred Fords built in time for distribution all over the country by December second, and lucky was the dealer, even in a large city, who had one to show. Most dealers had nothing more than some 18" x 24" pictures of the new car to show, and they made the most they could of these (SEE FIG. 27).

In addition to the pictures, dealers in some medium-sized cities actually had appointments for one-hour showings of the MODEL A as teams of Ford men drove exhibition cars from city to city on tight schedules!

While there were some who always believed Henry Ford could easily build a better car than Model T, practically none believed he could do it at as low a price. Everyone, therefore, was amazed that the MODEL A Tudor Sedan was priced at $495, the same as Model T, and that the Roadster at $385 was only $25 more than the Model T of 1927.

Even the knowledgeable Ford executives were amazed! About this, Lawrence Sheldrick had this to say: "Edsel and Crawford tried awfully hard to determine the cost of the new Ford, but Henry Ford paid little attention. He just priced it to suit himself—I don't know what formula he used for that." Apparently Mr. Ford was willing to take a loss on initial sales* of the new car, relying on increased volume and later economies in manufacturing to transform MODEL A into a profit-maker. He did turn his $72,000,000 loss in 1928 into a $92,000,000 profit in 1929!

The Ford dealers already had 500,000 orders on their books for MODEL A before the national showing. After that the attractive Fords at their unbelievably low prices induced such a flood of new orders from Ford-starved customers that Henry Ford advised his dealers to take no more orders until May of 1928! Production just couldn't get rolling fast enough to meet the orders already written.

Many Ford dealers suffered heavy losses as they waited for cars. They took some comfort from the resignation of the detested sales manager, William A. Ryan, and the coming of the more considerate Fred L. Rockelman; but even he couldn't help much. Uneven distribution of new Ford cars throughout the nation was inevitable, and many dealers were accusing even Rockelman of "playing favorites."

*Losses on the initial MODEL As were later found to be $320 for the Tudor, and $335 for the Phaeton.

Actually, many prominent people were given preference in new car deliveries. We already noted that W. Averell Harriman got the first MODEL A in New York. Then Senator James Couzens of Michigan was given MODEL A No. A35, the same serial number as his first Model A of 1903. Douglas Fairbanks and Mary Pickford were delighted to obtain an early Ford Coupe, and Princess Ileana of Roumania, Carl Sandburg, and Franklin D. Roosevelt all received early cars. But by spring, all this favoritism had to stop in order to bring peace to the ranks of the dealers.

By March, 1928, production was up to about 2,000 cars per day, and by mid-year, was up to 8,000 per day. The initial rush was over, the "man in the street" who had waited for Ford's new car could at last buy one, and the MODEL A had already become a national fixture. Now it remained only for Ford to increase production still more and to decrease costs. He did both, and by 1929, MODEL A had forged far ahead of all other makes.

But what of Chevrolet during this time? Hadn't this car hastened the end of Model T, then wrested leadership from Ford. Certainly not according to the records.*

Passenger car output of the industry in 1927 was a little more than 3,000,000 cars. This was almost 1,000,000 less than the 1926 output. But since Ford production alone dropped by more than 1,000,000 cars, the change from a 4,000,000 to a 3,000,000 car year was due *solely* to the disappearance of the Model T.

The fact is, *nobody* sold the cars that Ford did not sell. Chevrolet sales did increase by about 220,000; but this was only one-fifth of the Ford decrease. And this Chevrolet increase was really at the expense of Willys and Durant sales—the other large producers in the "under $700" field. Actually, there were nearly 800,000 fewer sales in the Ford-Chevrolet price class in 1927 than in 1926. This, then, was the number of people who chose to buy no other car in 1927 but to wait for the "new Ford"—whatever it might be! The popular belief today that Chevrolet captured the Ford customers with the ending of Model T is a myth.

As in any automobile race, Henry Ford's "pit stop," to retool for MODEL A, allowed the second car to lead the pack temporarily. But, with the coming of MODEL A, Henry Ford soon resumed his leadership in the industry. In 1929 he produced half again as many cars as Chevrolet made; and in 1930, the first year of the "great depression," he built 1,485,600 MODEL A Fords or twice as many cars as Chevrolet made! In those "hard times," Ford was selling 42.5% of *all* cars and trucks made in the United States—a record almost as good as his best years with the Model T. MODEL A had come to stay.

*Reference: *The Automobile Industry*, E. D. Kennedy, 1941.

George Haberfelde, Inc., Bakersfield, Calif.

The first Model A's were snapped up so fast that many dealers lacked even one car for display. Here is typical 1927 introduction built on photos, flags, and speeches

FIGURE 29. A DEALER WITH NO FORDS!

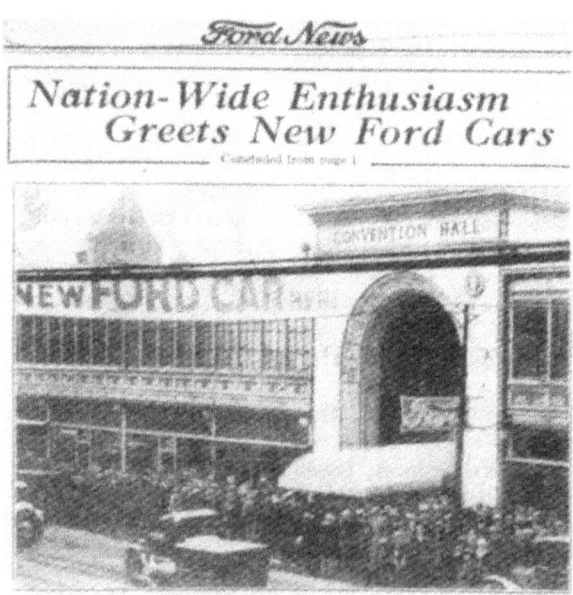

Clipping courtesy Research and Information Dept., Ford Motor Company.

FIGURE 31. NATION-WIDE ENTHUSIASM GREETS NEW FORD CARS.

CHAPTER VII
EVOLUTION

"Revolution" was Henry Ford's awesome term for his disturbing experience of change-over from Model T to MODEL A. He never expected to repeat it; rather, he expected MODEL A to remain the standard Ford product fuly as long as did Model T. But what Henry Ford did not realize was that, while Model T, at creation, had been nearly twenty years ahead of its time, MODEL A was actually but a timely compromise, albeit a good one. That it continued as a successful—even a formidable—contender in the changing automotive world for those four years was a tribute more to its dependability and stamina than to its modernity. There was yet another factor favoring MODEL A then, its high quality at low price. This was the answer for the man caught in the economy squeeze of the "great depression" but who still wanted a good, *new* car.

Henry Ford knew that in the continued production of MODEL A he would have to make many small and gradual alterations for, after all, the car had gone directly from the drawing room into production. These expected changes he called "evolution." Evolution never disturbed him nor his plant; evolution he could control and turn to advantage; evolution enabled him to effect improvements and economies. And evolve is just what MODEL A did.

What interests us now are some of the more relevant of the nearly 5,000 minor and the 150 major changes made to MODEL A from its beginning on October 21, 1927 to its end on April 30, 1932—changes which in number fell just short of equaling MODEL A's 5,500 parts!

So standardized was MODEL A that only one major body style change was made, and that in the 1930 Fords. Ford officially recognized no change between the 1928 and 1929 cars—but the changes were many and minute. Ford did recognize a change between the 1930 and 1931 cars—but the changes were few and faint. Consequently, a passing MODEL A can only be identified *quickly* as either the 1928-29 style (SEE FIG. 46)—as characterized by its low hood and nickel radiator shell, its reverse curved cowl and coupé pillar, and its 21" wheels—or the 1930-31 style (SEE FIG. 44)—distinguished by its high hood, its stainless steel radiator shell, it smooth, tapered cowl, and its 19" wheels with the larger hub caps. More positive identification requires closer examination; most of the prominent, *general* features peculiar to each style year are summarized briefly here, then considered in more detail:

MODEL A FORDS — SOME PROMINENT GENERAL CHARACTERISTICS OF EACH STYLE YEAR				
	1928	**1929**	**1930**	**1931**
Head Lamps	Nickel, "acorn".	Nickel, "acorn", "Twolite".	Stainless, parabolic, "Twolite".	Same.
Head Lenses	Vertical flutes.	Vertical flutes with prisms.	Same.	Same.
Tail Lamp(s)	Nickel, cylindrical, "Duolight", forged bracket.	Nickel, cupped, "Duolamp", pressed steel bracket.	Stainless, cupped, "Duolamp", pressed steel bracket.	Same.
Radiator Shell	Nickel, low & rounded, 13/16" wire holes, teardrop tab on crank hole cover, blue enamel emblem.	Nickel, low & rounded, 15/16" wire holes, dumbbell tab on crank hole cover, blue enamel emblem.	Stainless, high, painted panel insert at bottom only. Blue enamel emblem.	Stainless, high, painted panel insert at bottom and at top. Pressed stainless emblem.
Bumpers	Nickel, reverse curved ends, **round** head on center bolt*.	Nickel, reverse curved ends, **oval** head on center bolt*.	Chromium, slight bow, all bolts capped with pressed stainless*.	Same.
Cowl	Reverse curved with coupe pillar, exposed fuel tank.	Same, (Except for Briggs & Murray bodies.)	High, tapered smoothly into hood, concealed fuel tank.	Same.
Steering Wheel	Red plastic, dished.	Black plastic, dished.	Black plastic, flat, large hub.	Same.
Dash Panel	Nickel, heart shaped. Oval speedometer.	Same.	Same. (Mid-year change to 1931 style.)	Stainless, oval, ribbed center, round speedometer.
Wheels & Tires	21 x 4.50.	Same.	19 x 4.75.	Same.
Running Boards	Separate, ribbed rubber, zinc trim.	Same.	**Integral** with splash apron, pyramid rubber, stainless trim.	**Separate**, pyramid rubber, stainless trim.
Splash Aprons	One piece.	Same.	Two piece.	One piece.

*Note that all bumper bolt heads had the depressed portions painted the same shade of blue as the porcelain enamel radiator emblem regardless of body color.

Photo courtesy Research and Information Dept., Ford Motor Company.

FIGURE 30. THE TWENTY MILLIONTH FORD.

Henry Ford's 20,000,000th car was this MODEL A Town Sedan 155-C which rolled off the Rouge assembly line on April 14, 1931. Its serial number was about A4,521,600. Visible distinctions between this car and the similar Fordor Sedan are the hand loops on the rear quarter window posts, and the cowl lamps, factory equipped.

The car is pictured here in front of the Henry Ford Museum, a reproduction of Philadelphia's famous Independence Hall. The Museum was dedicated October 21, 1929, by Thomas A. Edison and Herbert Hoover.

The "Twenty Millionth Ford" was proudly lettered not only on the sides but even on the roof, attesting to Henry Ford's air-mindedness.

THE 1928 MODEL A FORDS

Body Model	Body Name	Weight pounds	Price	Illustrations
35-A	Standard Phaeton	2140	395	Figs. 11, 13, 40
40-A	Standard Roadster	2050	385	Figs. 1, 21, 82
45-A	Standard Coupe	2200	495	Fig. 47
49-A	Special Coupe	2200	500	Fig. 47
50-A	Sport Coupe	2265	550	
54-A	Business Coupe	2285	495	Fig. 89a
55-A	Tudor Sedan	2340	495	Figs. 27, 45, 95a
60-A	Fordor Sedan (Briggs)	2467	570	Figs. 4, 49, 77
76-A	Roadster Pick-up Truck	2073	395	Fig. 69

By January MODEL A production was really underway and the inevitable process of evolution began. Let us follow, month-by-month, the more interesting and important of the many changes made in the new Fords:

January, 1928.

About 5,000 MODEL A Fords had been built with the single brake system before threats of adverse state legislation forced Henry Ford to introduce the separate, extra parking brake equipment. This major change resulted in completely obsoleting the original "AR" type brake drum, backing plate, hub, wheel, wheel lugs, and hub cap. The new rear brake drum was changed from a single to a dual drum and the new "B" type wheel was made with a larger lug plate to fit over the new "B" type rear brake drum. The old style hub cap, which closely resembled the Model T cap with the hexagonal bead around the outer edge, was enlarged and the outer bead made circular. The Model T type forged wheel lug, which had a tapered shoulder larger in circumference than the hexagonal shank itself, was changed to the less expensive lug we know today. This new lug was simply turned from "hex" stock to make a rounded head and a tapered bearing surface against the lug plate of the wheel.

The new "B" type wheels and drums then remained unchanged for the duration of the MODEL A; it is important never to interchange the "AR" and "B" wheels and drums because of the resulting improper supporting of wheels on mismated drums.

With the change in the brake system, the hand lever was relocated from the left of the frame to a position directly in front of the gear shift lever. The opening thus left in the side of the body floor was covered by a plate at first screwed into place, then riveted in place. By mid-year, the hole was eliminated.

Earliest of the MODEL A Fords had the old Model T type bumpers without an end bolt; these were soon changed to the familiar type.

The Phaeton and Roadster (and Roadster Pick-up) were first fitted with outside door handles about this time.

February, 1928.

While the heavy trucks were still designated as MODEL AA, the stamping of the "AA" prefix on the engine block numbers was discontinued with the adoption then of the same type clutch spring in all engines. Thereafter, all engine numbers had only the "A" prefix.

The riveting of the splash pan within the oil sump pan was discontinued; the splash pan was then held in place by being snapped into grooves in the sides of the oil pan.

May, 1928.

MODEL A production was at last in full swing at about 8,000 cars per day (the all-time high for MODEL A production was 9,100 on June 26, 1929).

Now the Briggs-built Fordor Sedan body (SEE FIG. 44) was added to the Ford line. It was more luxurious than the other bodies and it eliminated the anular "coupé pillar" by introducing the concealed fuel tank under the tapered cowl--this styling was to become the outstanding mark of all the 1930-31 Fords. The Fordor had nickeled moulding at the juncture of hood and cowl, and the cowl itself had a ventilator door in the side. The rear upper quarter was "blind" and covered with leather while the top was a Seal Brown fabric.

The Business Coupe was a new body which resembled the Sport Coupe with a fabric covered rear quarter but without the Landau irons of the Sport Coupe.

While early Ford catalogs showed a four door Ford having the coupé pillar and reverse curved cowl just like the Tudor model, this body style was never produced as a Sedan, but it did appear later as a taxicab.

Genuine accessories introduced this month were windshield wings and top boots for the open cars.

July, 1928.

During this month two new makes of "ah-ooga" horns were added to the original Sparton—the E. A. and the Ames. For a while these had three different horn motor covers; later all were standardized.

More genuine Ford accessories included a spare wheel lock, a Boyce motometer bearing the Ford emblem, and the first of the "quail" radiator cap ornaments. The quail cap later became the mark of the 1930-31 Ford Roadsters and Phaetons in particular.[*]

---

[*]Luther H. Killam of Durham, Conn., uncovered the story behind the "winged quail" ornament. In a letter to Luther, Glen A. Johnson of the Stant Manufacturing Company, Incorporated, of Connersville, Ind., stated:

"It might interest you to know that the writer designed and modeled this ornament as one of his first projects for Stant. We secured live quail from the Indiana Conservation Department, and built special padded cages for them as they beat themselves to death against wood or metal screening. We photographed them in all positions and measured them to get complete records before returning them to the Conservation Department. We made models in clay, wax, and finally brass from which Ford gave approval. Diecasting dies were then engraved to match exactly the master brass model and hundreds of thousands were run from these dies.

The ornament was produced as a service item for a number of years after production of MODEL A was stopped. An added note and the part we do not like is the fact that Ford ordered these dies scrapped a number of years ago."

August, 1928.

Landau irons were made available as accessories for imparting a "sporty look" to the Business Coupes already on the road, and detailed instructions for installing the irons were furnished all dealers.

The Briggs Body Company was by this time supplying about 2,500 bodies daily to Ford and the Murray Body Company was just beginning to fill Ford orders for more bodies.

A "Special Coupe" was introduced; this was exactly like the first coupe (45-A) except the Special Coupe (49-A) had the rear top quarter covered with black leather.

September, 1928.

The original two-piece venturi tube in the Zenith carburetor was changed to a one-piece tube.

A lubrication fitting was added on the top of the steering sector shaft near the frame of the car.

The original type pointer with numerals were omitted from the shock absorbers.

October, 1928.

Henry Ford's troublesome Abell starter drive with its flimsy ½" drive shaft was obsoleted and succeeded by the standard Bendix drive having a ⅝" drive shaft. These two starter mechanisms were not interchangeable in any way.

The removable, round plate in the bottom of the oil pan under the oil pump was eliminated.

November, 1928.

The five-bearing cam shaft was replaced by a three-bearing shaft and the engine block was altered accordingly. These two different cam shafts were interchangeable in either block.

The red plastic steering wheel was replaced by black plastic which didn't rub off onto the driver when wet, as did the red!

The four-point engine mounting was changed to a three point system with a "floating" front supporting yoke. For this the two original upward-projecting tabs were cut off the front cross member and a forged yoke supported on two small springs was substituted. (Later parts suppliers offered very good rubber pads in place of the two springs on top of the cross member and the one spring under it.)

A new solid "oil-less" brake cross shaft was installed to eliminate the original lubricated type—in the interest of manufacturing economy.

At about engine number 560,000, the troublesome multiple-disc clutch (patterned after the Lincoln clutch in all but performance!) and its flywheel were obsoleted by the new, improved single-disc clutch assembly. Many an early 1928 Ford later had the new type clutch installed by the owners or their dealers. The difficulty with the multiple-disc clutch lay in the fact that the discs were thick sheet metal gears having fine teeth fitted into mating internal gear teeth in the deep flywheel. As the clutch facings dusted off with wear, the dust was compacted by centrifugal force into the roots of the internal gear teeth. This plugged them up and trapped the "floating" clutch discs so that, one by one, they ceased to release. Then all the power was transmitted by the one, last disc which soon wore out. This never happened with the single-disc clutch assembly.

December, 1928.

The lower "leg" was added to the choke lever at the butterfly valve to permit attaching a wire to run through the radiator for operating the choke when cranking.

By this time the 5-brush "Powerhouse" generator was no longer furnished on any of the engines. The less troublesome, more conventional 3-brush generator had already become standard for the duration of MODEL A.

The official showing of the 1929 Fords was in January and, though Henry Ford did not announce any "changes" in the 1929 Fords, he did introduce many new body styles.

Photo by Kenneth Stauffer, AACA Photographer.

FIGURE 32. THE BABY LINCOLN.

Of all the MODEL A Fords, none so closely resembles the contemporary Lincoln as does this 1929 Town Sedan 155-A. In designing this luxurious Ford, Edsel borrowed freely and well from his Lincoln creation *(see also Figs 2 and 3)*.

Note the smaller oval escutcheon bolt in the center of the bumper; in 1928 it was round with the FORD script in its center. Regardless of body color, all MODEL A escutcheon bolts were painted the same bright blue as the enameled radiator emblem.

This is a photograph of the author's car at the Hershey (Pa.) Meet in 1958.

FIGURE 33. 1929 STATION WAGON — "LIKE HAVING AN OLD FRIEND BACK!"

Owned and restored by Howard G. Henry, North East, Md.

To their fine collection of antique Packards, the Howard Henrys added this recently restored 1929 Ford Station Wagon, 150-A, just because it is the exact duplicate of Howard's first MODEL A. Now they take great pleasure in driving it to AACA Meets as well as running errands about their Piney Creek dairy farm where their four young boys can drive it on the private roads. Mrs. Henry also prefers the MODEL A for driving the children to the school bus.

One of the few "genuine" Ford factory-built station wagons, it was assembled on June 11, 1929 and carries the Murray Body No. M250 3569. It is finished in the original Manila brown hood and cowl, varnished maple body, and black fenders and chassis. Howard chose cream color for the wheels.

Mr. Henry purchased the car from its second owner for $200 in 1958 and spent an additional $392.31, plus family labor, in its restoration. The car was completely dismantled, then rebuilt like new. With the exception of only three pieces of new maple, the entire body is original. In spite of the hours spent in cleaning, scraping, rubbing, and painting, the Henrys consider the project both rewarding and educational for the whole family. They and all their friends are amazed at the pep and power of the rejuvenated 30-year-old MODEL A.

THE 1929 MODEL A FORDS

Body Model	Body Name	Weight pounds	Price	Illustrations
35-A	Standard Phaeton	2140	440	Figs. 6, 83
40-A	Standard Roadster	2050	435	Fig. 8
45-A	Standard Coupe	2200	500	Fig. 47
49-A	Special Coupe	2200	510	Fig. 47
50-A	Sport Coupe	2265	530	Fig. 52
54-A	Business Coupe	2225	490	Fig. 89a
55-A	Tudor Sedan	2340	500	Fig. 46
60-A	Fordor Sedan (Briggs) Leather Back, Seal Brown Top	2386	600	Fig. 87a
60-B	Fordor Sedan (Briggs) Leather Back, Black Top	2386	600	Fig. 87a
60-C	Fordor Sedan (Briggs) Steel Back	2386	600	
68-A	Cabriolet	2339	645	Fig. 86a
135-A	Taxi Cab	2500	800	Fig. 65
140-A	Town Car	2500	1200	Figs. 61, 62
150-A	Station Wagon	2482		Figs. 9, 22, 23, 33, 88a
155-A	Town Sedan (Murray)	2475	670	Figs. 5, 32, 53, 70
155-B	Town Sedan (Briggs)	2475	670	Fig. 3
165-A	Standard Fordor Sedan (Murray) (3-window)	2462	625	
165-B	Standard Fordor Sedan (Briggs) (3-window)	2462	625	
170-A	Standard Fordor Sedan (2-window)	2467	625	

(Commercial line not listed here.)

January, 1929.

Among the new Fords for 1929 was the taxi cab. This has the "coupé pillar" characteristic of the Tudor Sedan and, perhaps, was the design originally intended for the Fordor cars in 1928 but never produced. Of course, the interior was especially dsigned for taxi service; the driver's seat was enclosed by a glass partition and a "jump" seat permitted a fourth person to ride in the rear compartment.

Most striking of the new Fords for 1929 was the Town Sedan (not to be confused with Town Car). This was an exceptionally luxurious four-door, 3-window sedan; the interior was quite roomy, the rear floor was dropped in the center, the upholstering was in rich Mohair with side arm rests and a pull-down center arm rest in the rear cushion. Nickeled cowl lamps were "standard" equipment, with trunk, trunk rack, and bumper extensions as optional equipment. Both Briggs and Murray built these bodies; the Murray-built Town Sedans had white metal cowl lamp brackets, while the Briggs had brass castings.

The Town Car was offered for those who wanted a car with both "snob appeal" and maneuverability and economy in afternoon down-town transportation. The chauffeur usually sat in the open although a snap-on fabric cover was provided for him.

The Station Wagon (built by Murray) was introduced later in the year and was another Ford "first" in that it was the first station wagon in the industry to be assembled in the factory; all other station wagons were more or less "custom built" on commercial chassis by independent body builders.

In spite of the many major engine changes made two months earlier, a few more were effected. A new, solid-skirt, light weight aluminum piston was adopted to replace the original split-skirt aluminum piston.

The timing gear cover plate was simplified by elimination of an external rib and the "timing pin" was changed from a hexagonal section to a square section.

The long, oval handle on the oil dip stick was changed to a small circular handle.

The starter switch pedal was made smaller and was screwed into the switch.

Finally, the shroud behind the radiator and around the fan, which added so much to the efficiency of the fan, was eliminated as a matter of economy. Many people mistakenly believed that the shroud reduced the flow of air through the radiator!

Advent of the 1929 models marked the beginning of a progressive replacement of the forged body and fender and lamp brackets with pressed steel brackets. Until June of 1929, there was often a mixture of both forged and pressed steel running board brackets on the same car, for instance!

February, 1929.

New "Twolite" head lamps were introduced this month along with the cup-shaped "Duolamp." The original one-bulb (21-3 CP) head lamps (parts A-13004-A and A-13005-A) were succeeded by either a two-bulb head lamp (A-13005-C) for body styles without cowl lamps, or a single-bulb type (A-13005-D) for cars with cowl lamps. The Twolite lamps had new lenses with prisms added to the former fluted type.

A new lighting switch was provided having an extra contact for the parking light bulb in the Twolite head lamp or for the cowl lamps on the Town Sedan.

The holes in the radiator shell were enlarged from $13/16$" to $15/16$" to permit the new three-wire cables and enlarged terminal plugs to pass through.

A percentage of the 1929 Fords were now being assembled with a new two-tooth steering gear sector which was fully adjustable for wear. Many months passed before the original seven-tooth gear sector assembly was completely obsoleted.

March, 1929.

The front wheel hubs were changed from expensive forgings to the pressed steel type; these remained standard for the duration of MODEL A.

Cowl lamps were offered through the dealers as accessories for installation on Fords not regularly equipped with them.

The flywheel web was increased in thickness from $3/8$" to $25/32$" where it mated with the crankshaft flange; longer cap screws were required thereafter for this flange.

April, 1929.

The rear main crankshaft bearing cap was changed from a forging to a casting, which had to be made larger to obtain necessary strength. The cap bolts were then lengthened accordingly from 3%" to $4\,3/16$". This change was one for manufacturing economy, as were all such changes from forgings to castings or stampings.

The fuel valve handle under the cowl tank was also changed from a forging to a pressed steel handle.

The entire throttle assembly (A-9725) was redesigned for simplicity and economy; the accelerator pedal shaft was changed from two- to one-piece construction (A-9734).

May, 1929.

To reduce tendency for engine to burn oil; the valve chamber cover was changed to lower the oil return pipe and thus lower the oil level in the valve chamber.

Spark plug gap specification was changed from .027" to .035".

June, 1929.

The new three-window Fordor Sedan, model 165-A and 165-B, was introduced this month. This model resembled the Town Sedan but had no cowl lamps nor luxurious interior.

The universal joint housing cap was changed by removing the extension lug which had served to support the torque tube on the center cross member during assembly before mounting the engine in the chassis.

July, 1929.

The engine valve guides were shortened from $2\,3/8$" to $2\,1/8$" to help prevent valve sticking.

The clutch release-arm fastening pins were increased in diameter so they would be strong enough to permit elimination of the former keys and keyways—this reduced manufacturing costs.

The cylinder block rear wall was reinforced inside the block.

A new breather pipe was installed on the crankcase which had four baffles sloping upward instead of downward in an attempt to reduce oil blow-by.

An oil hole was made in the starting crank bearing to permit lubricating the front spring within the cross member.

A second type of head lamp plug and socket (A-14584-C and A13075-B) were introduced which obsoleted the original part (A-13075-AR).

The hand brake lever was moved from its position in front of the gear shift lever to the right side of the gear shift lever.

August, 1929.

Electric windshield wiper motors were replaced by the vacuum type starting in the Tudor Sedans and gradually extending to all body types by July, 1930. The intake manifold was now drilled and tapped for a vacuum hose connection.

October, 1929.

A larger water passage was provided in the center of the cylinder block, head, and head gasket. The new type head gasket could be used on the older engines.

November, 1929.

The oil pump body was changed from a forging to a casting and the shank was then ribbed for strength. The pump shaft and brushing size was increased from $21/32$" to $3/4$".

The front fender pressed steel bracket was changed to give more tire clearance. Only two vertically-spaced bolts and holes were used for attaching the new bracket instead of the former three.

FIGURE 34. YESTERDAY'S PILE OF JUNK.

Mrs. Gerrits ruefully views the remains of a 1931 Ford De Luxe Roadster in a Wisconsin junkyard and wonders if her husband really should have saved it from the doom of an open hearth furnace.

Russell J. Gerrits, of Chicago, thought so in 1954 and devoted several years of work to its restoration. At first made only roadworthy, the car did not satisfy Russell until he had completely rebuilt it—twice! The finished car now an AACA National First Prize winner, appears in Figure 35.

FIGURE 35. TODAY'S PRIDE AND JOY.

*1931 Ford De Luxe Roadster 40-B, owned and restored by
Russell J. Gerrits, Chicago, Ill.*

No pile of junk this, but a beautifully and authentically restored MODEL A No. 4316729. Twice a first place winner in MARC meets at Ford's Greenfield Village in 1955 and 1957, it was re-restored in 1958 in time to be judged a National First Prize winner by AACA at the Lake Forest (Ill.) Meet.

The color is Washington blue and Tacoma cream; the upholstering is tan leather. Note the authentic and very popular "quail" mascot on the radiator cap.

FIGURE 36. IT CAN BE RESTORED!

Harold G. Fulmer and his two sons found this discouraging looking relic on a farm near their home in Allentown, Pa. Although new to the hobby and complete amateurs, they restored this 1928 Ford Station Wagon to prize-winning condition at a cost of only $565.98—and plenty of their own labor!

Figure 37 shows the car in process of restoration; Figure 38 shows the completed car.

FIGURE 37. READY TO REBUILD A MODEL A.

Harold G. Fulmer has all the metal parts for his 1928 Ford Station Wagon spread out in preparation for reassembly. Each piece has been cleaned, inspected, and repaired or replaced prior to prime-painting. This is the accepted method of restoring a MODEL A. (See Fig. 36 for a view of the original condition of the car, and Fig. 38 for a view of the restored car).

FIGURE 38. 1928 FORD — CUSTOM BUILT STATION WAGON.

Owned and restored by Harold G. Fulmer, Allentown, Pa.
(Engine No. A210759)

Originally one of the 1928 Ford Commercial Chassis fitted outside the Ford plant with a "custom built" station wagon body, this car was excellently restored, piece by piece, from the rotted relic shown in Figure 36. All work except electroplating and spray painting was done by the owner and his two sons, all of whom were complete amateurs.

Note the unusual arrangement for rolling up the side curtains and fastening them with little straps along the edge of the roof.

This car has already won several prizes in the AACA Lehigh Valley Region and at other local Meets.

FIGURE 39. AN AUTHENTIC RESTORATION.

Owned and restored by John A. Mearkle, Springfield, Pa.
(Engine No. A4181349)

This early 1931 Standard Roadster, 40-B, displays the AACA National First Prize winner emblem (next to the left head lamp) which distinguishes it as an outstanding and authentic restoration. Most remarkable is the fact that, before restoration, the car was an almost hopelessly rusted-out hulk.

Body is blue, fenders and running gear are black, wheels and stripe are cream. Note the stainless steel radiator shell with painted inserts both top and bottom; this is the principal external feature distinguishing the 1931 Fords.

Photo by Duane Fielding, Prospect Park, Pa.

FIGURE 40. A LATE 1928 FORD PHAETON.

Audie, Les, and Charlie Henry appear in their 1928 Ford Phaeton 35-A enroute to the MARC Holiday Hill (Conn.) Meet where the Phaeton took first place in the 1954 competitions. A National First Prize winner at the AACA Granville (Ohio) Meet in 1955, it won first again in the Senior division at the AACA Ithaca (N.Y.) Meet in 1956, and has been a consistent winner at Regional meets.

Built late in 1928 (Serial No. A650684), this Phaeton was factory equipped with the improved single disc clutch. All other 1928 features are unchanged: it has the cylindrical tail lamp, red steering wheel, light brown upholstering, "power house" generator, hand brake (squeeze type) directly in front of gear lever, the little round Ford escutcheon bolt in center of front bumper, and the vertically fluted head lamp lenses.

Arabian sand body with seal brown mountings, and black fenders, wheels, and running gear are authentic for this car.

Photo courtesy The Atlantic Refining Company.

FIGURE 41. CARS LINING UP FOR GREATEST SHOW ON EARTH.

The largest gathering of antique cars in the world is found annually in the Hershey, Pa. stadium as guests of the Hershey Chocolate Company. Now MODEL A Fords frequently number nearly 60 of the more than 700 cars of all ages and makes at the annual Fall Meet of the Antique Automobile Club of America. (See also Fig. 71.)

THE 1930 MODEL A FORDS

Body Model	Body Name	Weight pounds	Price	Illustrations
35-B	Standard Phaeton	2212	440	Fig. 54
40-B (Std.)	Standard Roadster	2200	450	Figs. 80, 90b
40-B (De Luxe)	De Luxe Roadster	2230	520	
45-B (Std.)	Standard Coupe	2257	495	Fig. 48a
45-B (De Luxe)	De Luxe Coupe	2265	545	Fig. 48b
50-B	Sport Coupe	2283	525	
55-B	Tudor Sedan	2375	495	Fig. 89b
68-B	Cabriolet	2273	625	Fig. 86b
140-B	Town Car (Same as in 1929)	2525	1200	
150-B	Station Wagon	2505	640	
155-C	Town Sedan (Murray)	2475	640	
155-D	Town Sedan (Briggs)	2475	640	
165-C	Standard Fordor Sedan (Murray)	2500	600	
165-D	Standard Fordor Sedan (Briggs)	2500	600	
170-B (Std.)	Standard Fordor Sedan (Briggs)	2500	600	Fig. 87b
170-B (De Luxe)	De Luxe Fordor Sedan (Briggs)	2988	640	Fig. 87b
180-A	De Luxe Phaeton	2285	625	Fig. 55
190-A	Victoria Coupe	2372	580	

January, 1930.

January again was the month for showing the new Ford models, and this time Henry Ford proudly announced there were major changes in the MODEL A. These were mostly in the new bodies which were better proportioned with higher hoods and radiators and with smoother cowls and body panels. Other changes included the use of chromium and stainless steel for radiator shell, lamps, and trim; new, larger "balloon" tires, size 4.75 x 19; shallower, "parabolic" shaped head lamp shells; slightly bowed bumper bars (chromium plated); and the flat steering wheel with a large hub. By this time, all the steering sector gears were of the two-tooth type and were fully adjustable for wear. Spark and throttle control rods were contained entirely within the steering column.

The radiator shells were stamped from stainless steel; because of the difficulty in deep-drawing the stainless steel and also for economy, the bottom panel was crimped in place and was painted instead of being highly polished.° The original style blue enameled radiator emblem remained, but the old style radiator cap with fluted edges and internal threads was replaced by a flat cap with knurled edge and with a quarter-turn interrupted screw for fastening. The fuel tank cap was also changed to match. Fenders were wider, lower and more graceful.

February, 1930.

The metal tube running from the terminal block to the generator cut-out as a conduit for the wires was changed to a pliable black lacquered loom. This was done because of complaints about breakage of the metal tube and because of frequent chafing of the wires and subsequent short-circuiting on the conduit.

The steering column was increased 1" in length and the column bracket was shortened ⅜" to provide easier steering and handling.

March, 1930.

The rear main bearing cap oil pipe was enlarged from 5/16" to ⅜" to permit quicker drainage of the oil in cold weather.

Rear engine supports were redesigned and made of heavier gauge pressed steel. Bolts used with the new supports were 1 17/32" long instead of 1⅞" as formerly.

The safety screen in the fuel tank hole was also made of heavier gauge metal and supplied with slots ½" deep (instead of only ⅜") for removing the screen without danger of it breaking.

The "stack" strap, used to hold the top in place when folded down, was now supplied as regular equipment on all roadsters.

° Joe Galamb, the designer, stated that the inserts were made of carbon steel to save the cost of stainless steel. Of course, carbon steel *had* to be painted to keep it from rusting.

Brake drums were improved by being rolled true and to finished dimensions instead of being ground to dimension as formerly. Rolling the drums produced a "worked hardened" surface which resists wear better than a ground surface. After this time, Ford recommended that customers buy new genuine Ford drums rather than having the old, worn drums remachined.

The former means for adjusting the parking brakes was discontinued; this saved manufacturing cost and Henry Ford believed parking brakes never needed adjustment in service.

Steering gear ratio was increased from 11¼ to 1 in the old gear to 13 to 1 in the new gear for easier turning of the steering wheel.

Artificial leather (cross Cobra grain) became optional upholstering material (trimming) for the Coupe and was suggested as being particularly attractive for Coupes used "for business purposes."

Brown mohair or deep tan Bedford cloth became the new optional upholstering material in the De Luxe Coupe, De Luxe Sedan, and the Town Sedan.

A dome light was now furnished in the De Luxe Coupe.

Spark plug gap specifications were increased from the range of .025" to .030" to the new range of .027" to .035".

April, 1930.

The generator shaft and pulley was changed by shortening the shaft and the hub. Old pulley hub length was 1 $^{5}/_{32}$"; new hub became $^{7}/_{8}$" long.

The emergency (parking) brake cross-shaft was changed from tubular to solid section.

The horn mounting bracket was widened from 1" to 1⅛" to fit the new head-lamp tie rods. The new bracket can be used on the old style rods with the "acorn" shaped head-lamps, but not vice versa.

May, 1930.

The breather pipe on the crankcase was changed for a third time to a pipe having three internal disc baffles with their centers bent downward, alternately left and right. This was the last attempt to check oil blow-by. (Owners solved this problem by installing an accessory flexible breather pipe to conduct oil vapors down below the car frame.)

Lubrication fittings were added to the water pump bushings and to the brake and clutch pedals.

The front shock absorber arms were offset to provide more clearance between arm and body. These new arms are interchangeable with the older style.

June, 1930.

A new body type was added: the De Luxe Phaeton. Having but two doors, a lowered steering wheel, and a lower, chromium plated windshield frame, this car presented a much sportier appearance than the four-door Standard Phaeton. The front seats folded forward to give access to the rear seat; all upholstering was in genuine leather with a two-tone grained effect. Regular equipment included cowl lamps; folding, chromium-trimmed rear trunk rack; one spare wheel mounted on the left side; rear view mirror on the windshield post; and a chromium-plated windshield wiper motor, *now vacuum operated on all open body types.*

Because of the lowered steering column, a bend was put in the accelerator-to-steering column rod (A-9742-B) to allow it to clear the starter push rod.

The familiar heart-shaped, satin-finish instrument panel with the oval speedometer was changed to a horizontal oval stainless steel panel having a ribbed center and a round speedometer.

A two-piece metal spare tire cover was offered as an accessory; this was enameled black and was available either with or without chromium trim.

August, 1930.

The De Luxe Roadster appeared this month as the fourth open body type in the Ford Line. Regular equipment on this was the same as on the De Luxe Phaeton except the rumble seat cushions which were upholstered in artificial leather to match the appearance of genuine leather of the front seat, and there was a spare wheel mounted on each side of the car. This was the only MODEL A Ford to have twin side-mounted spare wheels as regular factory equipment; all other twin mountings were either on special order to the factory or were added by the dealers after delivery.

A new emergency brake lever assembly with finer ratchet teeth became standard for all Fords; this permitted finer adjustment of parking brake tension and easier release of the brake handle.

Bumper bars were reduced in length from 62⅞" (A-17757-C) to 60" (A-17757-D). This dimension is measured as the chord of the bumper arc, not along the face of the bumper bar.

Valve spring (A-6516-A1) was changed from 3$^{7}/_{16}$" free length to 2$^{15}/_{16}$" free length (A-6513-A2).

November, 1930.

The graceful Victoria Coupe, with the "bustle back" (which was luggage space reached from behind the rear seat cushion) was another completely new body type. Added this month to the Ford line, it was the first closed MODEL A to have a slanting windshield, to have no sun visor, and to have a *deep* drop in the floor to permit a lowered roof and silhouette. The Victoria Coupe bodies having a fabric-covered rear top quarter were made by the Briggs Company; those with the steel rear top quarter were made by Murray.

These three new bodies, the Victoria Coupe, the De Luxe Phaeton, and the De Luxe Roadster, were brought out by Ford in an attempt to capture those customers who normally would have purchased medium- or high-priced cars but whose income or budget had shrunk with the deepening of the current economic "depression."

Reversing the former trend, Ford changed the front fender brace from a steel stamping to a forging because of fatigue cracking of the pressed steel bracket where it was bolted to the car frame.

Photo courtesy Ford Motor Company.

FIGURE 42. 1930 FORD SPORT PHAETON (Special).

One of Edsel's body creations, this special "double cowl" Phaeton closely resembles the contemporary British sports car, Bentley. The American public was never favored with any MODEL As like this.

Photo by Kenneth Stauffer, AACA Photographer.

FIGURE 43. WORLD'S LARGEST MODEL A COLLECTION.

Not a used car lot of the '30s, as it may seem, but just a part of the private collection of more than 150 MODEL A and Model T Fords owned by Wayne Steinmetz of Stowe, Pa. Wayne, who believes "the MODEL A will come back," is still finding them and adding them to his collection. As a hobbyist, he is loath to part with any of his collection but he does help out friends who may need some new or used parts.

THE 1931 MODEL A FORDS

Body Model	Body Name	Weight pounds	Price	Illustrations
35-B	Standard Phaeton	2212	435	Figs. 7a, 7b, 51, 79
40-B (Std.)	Standard Roadster	2155	430	Fig. 39
40-B (De Luxe)	De Luxe Roadster	2230	475	Figs. 34, 35, 63, 64, 80, 81
45-B (Std.)	Standard Coupe	2257	490	
45-B	De Luxe Coupe	2265	525	
50-B	Sport Coupe	2283	500	
55-B	Tudor Sedan	2375	490	
68-B	Cabriolet	2273	630	Fig. 95c
68-C	Cabriolet	2273	630	Fig. 92
150-B	Station Wagon	2505	625	
155-C	Town Sedan (Murray)	2475	630	Fig. 30
155-D	Town Sedan (Briggs)	2475	630	
160-A	Standard Fordor Sedan	2462	590	
160-B	Town Sedan	2475	630	Figs. 94, 95b
160-C	De Luxe Fordor Sedan	2488	630	
165-C	Standard Fordor Sedan (Murray)	2462	590	
165-D	Standard Fordor Sedan (Briggs)	2462	590	
170-B	De Luxe Fordor Sedan (Briggs)	2488	630	Fig. 93
180-A	De Luxe Phaeton	2285	580	
190-A	Victoria Coupe	2372	580	Figs. 60, 88b, 91
400-A	Convertible Sedan		640	Figs. 66, 67, 77, 95d

For the 1931 MODEL A, Henry Ford claimed no change in models. As we have already noted, the only apparent changes involved merely the addition of a painted panel inserted at the top of the stainless steel radiator shell, substitution of a pressed stainless steel emblem for the former enameled plaque; and a return to the separate running board and the one-piece splash apron. Many of the 1931 sedans appeared this year with a visorless windshield.

On December 7, 1931, Henry Ford's revolutionary "en bloc" V-8 engine in Edsel Ford's new body styles appeared as the new Ford line for 1932. But MODEL A was continued in production until April 30, 1932, when the Model B Ford was announced.

Model B had the graceful body of the all-new V-8 Fords, but retained the Model A engine modified by the addition of a camshaft-operated fuel pump and by the addition of a centrifugally operated spark advance in the distributor. Following the Model B engine came a Model C which found application in several commercial chassis in the 1933 Ford line.

Henry Ford's V-8 engine was twenty years ahead of the rest of the industry in design, and for sheer numbers of these engines manufactured, none can even begin to equal the Ford production.

Photo courtesy Ford Motor Company.

FIGURE 44. THE FAMILY SEDAN IN 1930.

This Tudor Sedan, 55-B, was the most popular of the entire Ford line, particularly as a "family sedan." With the windshield open, as shown, air not only came directly in but was directed down to the floorboards by the cleverly shaped interior cowl panel or "facia board."

Photo by Kenneth Stauffer, AACA Photographer.

FIGURE 45. 1928 TUDOR SEDAN — MOST POPULAR IN ITS DAY.

This early MODEL A, No. 65617, was delivered in March of 1928 when production was still getting under way. Few but the very favored customers could get any MODEL A at all, then.

This Sedan 55A is partially restored in its original colors of Niagara blue body with black fenders and running gear.

The present owner is AACA member Walter Crew, Chadds Ford, Pa.

Photo by Utzy, Jenkinstown, Pa.

FIGURE 46. "A GOOD JUDGE OF OLD CARS."

Judge George C. Corson of Plymouth Meeting, Pa., a vice president of AACA and long a MODEL A enthusiast, recently restored this beautiful 1929 Ford Tudor Sedan, 55-A. Judge Corson took the car completely apart for cleaning, inspection, painting and nickel plating but, since it had been driven only 14,000 miles, no mechanical replacements were required to restore it to first class condition.

Ford recognized no style change between the 1928 and 1929 Fords (see Fig. 45); the only feature here visible which marks this car as a 1929 Ford is the cup-shaped tail lamp mounted on the rear fender with a pressed steel bracket (compare with Fig. 47).

Photo courtesy Research and Information Dept., Ford Motor Company.

FIGURE 47. THE NEW FOR COUPE FOR 1928.

When Henry Ford offered the 1928 Ford Coupe, 49-A, to the public, he expected to continue producing MODEL A unchanged for many years to come—just as he had done with Model T. Consequently it may be difficult to distinguish between this coupe and the 1929 coupe (also designated 45-A) which followed. These are also known as the Standard 5-window Coupe.

Aside from a slight change in shades, the colors remained the same blue, gray, tan, and green. The only *quick* way to identify this MODEL A as a 1928 is by its cylindrical tail lamp mounted on a forged bracket on the body. In 1929 the tail lamp was cup-shaped and was mounted on a pressed steel bracket on the fender.

Photo courtesy Research and Information Dept., Ford Motor Company.

FIGURE 48-A. THE STANDARD FORD COUPE FOR 1930.

Distinctly different in body lines from the 1928-29 Fords, this 1930 Coupe, 45-B, is typical of the more graceful design of the "second series" MODEL A cars. Just as the "first series" were essentially alike, so were the 1930 and 1931 Fords.

A quick way to identify this as a 1930 Ford is by its stainless steel radiator having a painted insert only at the bottom—the 1931 Ford had an insert both top and bottom. Generally, also, the two-piece splash apron (with running board integral with the main section of the apron) is a characteristic peculiar to the 1930 Ford.

Early 1930 Fords had the satin-finish nickel instrument panel, the same as the 1928-29 Ford (see Fig. 75), while the later ones had the smaller, flatter stainless steel, ribbed type in common with the 1931 Fords (see Fig. 77).

Photo courtesy Ford Motor Company.

FIGURE 48-B. 1930 DE LUXE FORD COUPE

The stainless steel cowl lamps and trim and the richer textured upholstering differentiates this De Luxe Coupe from the Standard Coupe. Both bodies are designated model 45-B, and the same body style prevailed for the 1931 Fords.

Photo by Kenneth Stauffer, AACA Photographer.

FIGURE 49. LATE 1928 FORD FORDOR SEDAN.

Owned by Clifford Jones, Spring City, Pa.

This distinguished looking 60-A Sedan, only recently restored to an authentic and beautiful condition, won First Prize at the 1958 MARC Ford Dix (N.J.) Meet.

This sedan, like all other sedans of the 1928-29 production, has a concealed fuel tank, larger engine hood, and a continuation of the body moulding along the cowl and hood to the nickel plated radiator shell. All bright work is nickel plated; fenders, wheels, and running gear are black; body is rose beige with seal brown mouldings. Tires are the original type Firestones.

Model A publicity photo with Wallace Beery and Emil Jannings also shows old Model T still hauling scenery in background

Clipping courtesy Research and Information Dept., Ford Motor Company.

Photo courtesy American Broadcasting Co., Hollywood, Calif.

FIGURE 51. THE REAL McCOYS!

Walter Brennan and MODEL A both star in the current television comedy series, "The Real McCoys," in which they combine with Dick Crenna and Kathy Nolan to depict an interesting and humorous facet of the American way of life. The 1931 MODEL A Phaeton is a "natural" choice of car for the part in these films, and lends an air of realism to the scenes as no other car could.

FIGURE 52. A PAIR OF "STARS" IN 1929.

Film star Dolores Del Rio was one of the first to own a new Ford "star" in 1929—the Sport Coupe model 50-A. Like other movie queens, Miss Del Rio set the style in sport cars and clothes for co-eds of America. Note the short skirt and cloche hat!

FIGURE 53. MODEL A CAMPER.

Camping trips off the beaten path with his first MODEL A were highlights of the author's college vacations. Les Henry is pictured here seated at his "kitchenette" trunk which opened to form a table, and exposed a refrigerator, pantry, and stove. The running board was fitted with a duffle locker, but the real "deluxe camping" feature added to his Town Sedan was a hinged front seat which made up into a comfortable bed.

There wasn't a mountain road in the eastern United States or Canada that MODEL A couldn't take in stride!

Photo by Kenneth Stauffer, AACA Photographer.

FIGURE 54. 1930 FORD STANDARD PHAETON.

This 1930 four-door Standard Phaeton, 35-B, has the chromium plated, folding windshield posts but, unlike the two-door De Luxe Phaeton, it has imitation grained leather upholstery and the spare tire is mounted on the rear.

Peculiar to most 1930 Fords is the one-piece running board and splash apron combination with a small, separate apron section ahead of the main unit—the resulting joint appears here in the apron as a line running down from the front door hinge. In 1931, Ford returned to the more practical separate running board and the one-piece splash apron.

Just beyond this Phaeton appears one of the last of the four-cylinder Fords, the 1932 Model B—an evolution from MODEL A. The graceful radiator shell and grill which, for the first time concealed the radiator core of Model B, was designed by Edsel Ford.

The striping on the hood louvres was not a factory item.

Photo courtesy Research and Information Dept., Ford Motor Company.

FIGURE 55. 1930 FORD DE LUXE PHAETON.

Production of this particularly graceful two door De Luxe Phaeton, 180-A, was started June 3, 1930. Color choice at first was limited to raven black with Aurora red wheels and stripe, and to Washington blue with Tacoma cream wheels and stripe. Upholstery was in genuine grained tan leather. De Luxe equipment included stainless steel cowl lamps, folding chromium plated windshield frame, chromium plated windshield wiper motor, and rear view mirror. A folding trunk rack with chromium trim was supplied on the rear and the one spare wheel was mounted on the left in a fender well.

World production of this 180-A Phaeton totaled 7,281 during 1930 and 1931.

Photo courtesy Research and Information Dept., Ford Motor Company.

FIGURE 60. THE ROUGE ASSEMBLY LINE IN 1931.

A Ford Victoria body, with drop-center floor, is lowered onto its chassis on the moving assembly line. Its fuel tank is entirely separate from the body and is concealed under the cowl. All brightwork, including the standard cowl lamp equipment, is stainless steel —"Allegheny metal"—except for the chromium plated bumpers.

The upper and lower painted portions of the radiator shell are carbon steel panels crimped into the stainless steel shell; this was one of "sheet metal Joe" Galamb's ideas for cutting production costs which appealed to the stylists, too. Note that a cheaper stainless steel stamping serves in place of the former blue enameled radiator emblem.

CHAPTER VIII
RESTORING MODEL A

MODEL A's present prestige and capability of inspiring pride of ownership can equal, if not surpass, that of any modern Detroit product—but only when the MODEL A is meticulously and *authentically* restored to "like new" condition. Anything less may be a nice automobile but it *cannot* be MODEL A!

Now, if you think you want to restore a MODEL A, first get one.* They can still be found today as wrecks in junkyards, as relics in old garages or barns, as grossly altered "old used cars" in daily use, or perhaps already restored in some degree. Prices will range from $15 for a junker to $1,600 for an *authentic* restoration.

When you find a MODEL A to restore, don't be discouraged by the hopeless appearance of a dismembered junker, nor fooled by the flashy appearance and paint of an unauthentically restored car. The latter will cost more to buy and has more work for you to *undo!*

Anybody can do *some* MODEL A restoration work himself; many amateurs have done it *all!* Certainly, anybody can do the first step himself—take the car *completely* apart. There is no half way—there is no easier way. The car *must* come apart so that each piece can be properly cleaned, inspected, repaired or replaced, refurbished and repainted like new, and then reassembled into a complete MODEL A.

Whether you are a beginner or not, it is always best to be systematic in dismantling a car for restoration. Keep related parts together in trays or boxes provided in advance; identify unfamiliar parts with tags or marks, and make brief sketches of their assembly, if necessary, so you can put them all back together properly later. Other aids in restoration may be found in Chapter XI, HELPFUL HINTS.

Usually it doesn't pay to rush through a restoration job—or any part of it. If you are temporarily stopped for the want of some part or specialized job you can't do, then set that work aside and take up another phase of the work. It is best to have several such jobs going at the same time so that, even if you have set yourself a deadline for completion, the overall restoration work can progress unhurried.

In every restoration project you will come across at least one problem that will seem insoluble and which may tend to discourage you to the point of giving up—don't! You quite probably can solve the problem with a little time and thought, or you will find someone who can solve it for you. In either case, the experience of having won out will give you immense personal satisfaction—like playing a hole-in-one on the golf course, or bowling a perfect game!

If you, personally, haven't the skill or equipment to weld, or to machine a part, or to paint the body, or to upholster, or to overhaul the engine and transmission—then get help from someone who can. Take such jobs to the local shops; there are many other restoration jobs you *can* do.

Remember always that *authenticity* is imperative—whether in a major item such as using only lacquer on the body and fenders of MODEL A, or whether in a minor item such as mounting the wheel on the spare rack with the valve stem at the top and with the FORD script in a horizontal, easily readable position! Trivial? Perhaps; but such were the details of MODEL A on the assembly line, and such are the details which must be preserved if we want a *real* MODEL A today. It is the attention paid to the trivial today which distinguishes a restoration job as authentic.

While higher quality restoration work is always encouraged, we must caution against "over-restoration." Examples of this may be seen on cars restored by the over-zealous in the form of chromium plated wheel lug nuts; filled, rubbed, and polished chassis and axles; fancy, plastic upholstery; striped engine hood louvres; and chromium plated engine parts. Any over-restoration is as bad as not enough—neither is authentic nor like the original MODEL A.

The accounts of the personal experiences of some of the AACA and MARC members who have recently restored MODEL A Fords are both interesting and illuminating:

Russell J. Gerrits, of Chicago, was brave enough to start with a pile of junk (SEE FIG. 34) "in a quite incomplete state, but in good, solid condition. At first the car was not restored to perfect condition; just given a complete but easy going-over in 1954. We had a very good time with the car during the summer, then it was gone over again for the MARC Meet in Dearborn in 1955, where it won first place. But I was certainly not entirely satisfied with the restoration, so in 1957 the car was again completely torn down and restored *to original* factory specifications (SEE FIG. 35). The chassis and motor were built up with as many *new* parts as possible purchased from Ford dealers or from club members dealing in parts. The car won again in the MARC and finally became the AACA National First Prize winner at Lake Forest in 1958."

Harold G. Fulmer of Allentown, Penna., is a recent AACA member who, as a complete amateur, successfully undertook restoration of the "relic" type of MODEL A. This was a project which included his two teen-age sons and about which he gives more detail: "Finally the boys came home from one of their many searches with the news that they had found a MODEL A Station Wagon. I went with them to look at it and all I could see was a rotted and rusted relic (SEE FIG. 33). It had been standing in a wooded area for twelve years, it had rifle shots through the hood, and it had a cracked cylinder head ... so we bought ourselves a lot of work ... for $15!"

The farmer who sold it couldn't figure out what they wanted with it and, after they had towed it home on borrowed wheels and with stops every block or so to pick up parts falling off the body, the neighbors wondered too. "Do you intend to make something out of *that?*" they asked.

Harold considered that a challenge, so he started: "I hosed it off and then took it all apart. Incidentally, we haven't a garage to work in—only a cellar with a 30-inch door. In the following weeks we bought a junk sedan as a parts car. *All* metal parts selected for the Station Wagon project were buffed down to the bare metal, washed in gasoline and taken into the cellar shop. Then each piece was carefully inspected, primed and painted, then made

---

*Of considerable help in finding and restoring a MODEL A is the book, *Buy An Antique Car*, written by Peg and Scott Bailey and published by Floyd Clymer.

up into sub-assemblies that would pass through the cellar door—front axle, rear axle, engine, frame, cowl, steering, etc.

"The body was rebuilt with the original type hard maple; the old pieces were first laid out on the floor to use as patterns. Fortunately, some of the pieces missing on one side happened to be on the other so we could duplicate all parts. We then set the frame on the axles and then used "C" clamps and a few bolts to assemble the wooden body as a temporary unit to make sure everything fit properly.

"A friend gave me an old treadle sewing machine which we used to sew up exact duplicates of the leatherette seat upholstering and the side curtains. These were made of convertible top material with plexiglas windows. We had to get an upholsterer to sew in the plexiglas because it was too stiff for our old sewing machine.

"Then one Saturday, the two boys and I took the car apart again and carried it outside; the rebuilt engine we skidded up the steps on the boys' sled (SEE FIG. 37). In another week we had the MODEL A reassembled and ready for the black and tan paint. So far, the restored car has won prizes in the AACA Lehigh Valley Region and at other local Meets."

Mr. Fulmer includes an itemized list of his restoration costs for this 1928 Ford Station Wagon:

COST OF RESTORING A 1928 FORD STATION WAGON
BY HAROLD FULMER AND SONS,
LEHIGH VALLEY REGION, AACA.

Description	Amount
Price of Station Wagon, November 1, 1957.	$ 15.00
Price of 1928 Ford Sedan parts car.	50.00
Maple wood to remake body.	76.72
New parts: muffler, timing gear, gaskets, windshield wiper, plugs, ignition parts, fan belt, water hose, etc.	47.49
Safety Plate glass windshield.	24.28
Black roof topping.	14.25
Curtain material, canvas, plexiglas, fasteners, etc.	64.12
Upholstering material, tacks, needles, thread.	33.35
Tires—3 new, 2 used.	64.29
*Chrome plating	45.05
(Original was nickel—AUTHOR'S NOTE)	
Rubber floor mats.	5.78
Paint brushes, nails, glue, varnish, paint remover, nails, screws, nuts, bolts, etc.	22.55
Running board material, counter top moulding, cement.	7.75
Battery and cables.	8.90
*Paint job on body.	89.00
Motometer and steering wheel.	3.00
Chrome plating on motometer, light switch, Ford emblem.	6.50
(Original was nickel—AUTHOR'S NOTE)	
Total expense	$578.03
Parts car sold for scrap (except motor, transmission and rear axle assembly).	− 12.05
Net cost of restoration.	$565.98

John Mearkle of Springfield, Penna., gives an account of his restoration of a 1931 Standard Roadster which became an AACA National First Prize winner at Pottstown in 1957 (SEE FIG. 39):

"I purchased the car on New Year's Eve, 1950 for seventy-five dollars. The car ran, and that is about all. The body was pretty well rusted out, badly dented and cracked. The rumble seat interior was in an advanced state of decay; the roof was a few tattered shreds of canvas over rotten bows; and the windshield frame was a rusted shell with no glass. The entire mess, as I found out later, was covered with five coats of house paint which actually served to hold some parts together!

"I did the restoration of the body myself, except for the roof, side curtains, and top bows. I made the windshield frame of ⅜" round brass stock, bent it to the shape of the cowl, and channeled it to take the glass and the 'T' rubber. Some of the small items, including one set of wing brackets, I made from solid brass stock by cutting, filing, and tapping where necessary. I had all of these items plus the bumpers and other bright work chromium plated.

The channeling supporting the body was so badly rusted through that I had to have new pieces made and welded onto the remaining solid body channel up near the front seat. The rumble seat floor and rear fender wells I made of sixteen gauge galvanized iron riveted into the original solid metal that remained after all the rusted portions were cut away.

"All dents were hammered out of the body, and all cracks were welded and reinforced from the inside. I filled in with solder all the places where I had welded and where I had pieced the body with galvanized iron. Then the entire body was filed and sanded as smooth as possible, and a coat of lacquer primer applied. The remaining small dents and ripples were filled in with lacquer putty and sanded again. The body and fenders were then sprayed with 14 coats of Ditzler lacquer—body color is Colony blue; fenders are jet black.

"The wheels were sandblasted, the spokes straightened, then painted with duPont Miami cream enamel. The frame, axles and under-portions of the body were painted with primer and two coats of black enamel. The engine, transmission, and all the running gear had been completely rebuilt using mostly new parts. I rebuilt the seat and sewed all the upholstery by hand—it took about four months for this, in my spare time.

"Total cost of this restoration (not including my labor) was about $1,800. I think this figure is rather high for a MODEL A, but I didn't pick out a car with reasonable restoring possibilities. Since restoration, I have driven the car 14,000 miles with no major repairs and I consider my restoration costs as money well spent!"

Of course the ultimate of all restoration work is to provide a desirable car to *drive* in addition to reactivating something of American automotive history. The restorer often refers to his efforts as "work" when actually it isn't all all—work is what you are doing when you would rather be doing something else! Just try to get an antique car restorer to do something else when he is in the midst of a restoration job and you'll find out whether or not he is working.

Hardly a collector will not admit that restoration "work" is as much a part of the fun as driving the finished car. The hobbiest who restores his first antique car —MODEL A or other—usually restores another; and then perhaps "just one more!" Nothing gives as much satisfaction as a restoration job well done, and the pride of ownership is enhanced by a pride of personal attainment and workmanship.

Most so-called "masculine" hobbies are strictly that, but MODEL A restoration is often a hobby for the whole family (SEE FIG. 33). The children can usually wield brushes with cleaning solvent on the mechanical parts, or with paint remover on the body, to good effect. And your wife might even take an interest in the trim and upholstering—particularly when she realizes that this way she at least has you home, albeit in the garage!

Of course, the finished car immediately becomes a vehicle of pleasure for the whole family—antique automobiling, particularly with others (SEE FIGS. 25, 41, 71 AND 84) is a new and thoroughly enjoyable family hobby and social activity.

For fullest enjoyment of the hobby you should join one of the many organizations devoted to antique automobiles in general and/or MODEL A Fords in particular. Through such affiliation you can receive help with your restoration work, information in the club magazine, and enjoyable association with kindred souls all enjoying this family hobby at meets, runs, picnics, back-country runs, cross-country tours, and regular social meetings.

It is impossible to list here all the numerous clubs catering to MODEL A enthusiasts, but we can, with propriety and no intent to slight any, list alphabetically those several clubs which are large enough to operate on a national basis with local Regional groups and which are large enough to publish regularly a recognized magazine or bulletin:

The Antique Automobile Club of America, Inc.
Hershey Museum, Hershey, Pa.

The Horseless Carriage Club of America, Inc.
7730 South Western Ave., Los Angeles 47, Calif.

The Model A Ford Club of America, Inc.
6924 San Fernando Road, Glendale, Calif.

The Model A Restorer's Club
P. O. Box 615, Zanesville, Ohio

The Veteran Motor Car Club of America
15 Newton Street, Brookline 46, Mass.

Photo courtesy Research and Information Dept., Ford Motor Company.

FIGURE 61.   1929 FORD TOWN CAR.

While not quite "formal" enough for the opera, this Town Car was ideal for morning or afternoon shopping or calling in the congestion of city traffic. A liveried chauffeur, thus exposed to the elements, afforded a definite distinction of class to the secluded passenger just as surely as if the car were a Rolls-Royce.

Only 1,197 of these 140-A bodies were built, many for European markets, and only in this 1929 style. Few remain in existence today, and these few are real collectors' items.

Photo courtesy Research and Information Dept., Ford Motor Company.

FIGURE 62.   1929 FORD TOWN CAR (140-A).

Priced at $1,200, the Ford Town Car had all the snob appeal of a Rolls-Royce but at one-tenth the cost. These special bodies were built, with slight variations, by both Murray and Briggs body companies. The rear compartment windshield was framed by a large aluminum casting. A canopy could be snapped into place over the chauffeur's seat for inclement weather use.

Photo by Kenneth Stauffer, AACA Photographer.

FIGURE 63. 1931 FORD DE LUXE ROADSTER — AFT.

Owned by John Lauer, this 1931 Ford De Luxe Roadster, 40-B, is shown at the 1957 Williams Grove Rally of the AACA Gettysburg Region. Features of this roadster are the rumble seat, side mounted spare wheels, full length rear bumper with a folding metal trunk rack finished in chromium trim, and a pair of stainless steel tail lamps.

The chromium plated bars behind the top are not handles but are brackets to support the top when folded down. The rear deck paint is protected from rubbing off the chromium rear window frame by four rubber buttons. Note the rumble seat step at right of bumper; a second step is on top of the fender.

Photo by Kenneth Stauffer, AACA Photographer.

FIGURE 64. 1931 FORD DE LUXE ROADSTER — FORE.

John Lauer's MODEL A De Luxe Roadster, 40-B, at the 1957 Williams Grove Rally. De luxe features in 1931 included the parabolic, stainless steel head lamps and cowl lamps; the chromium plated windshield frame; and twin side mounted wheels. The upholstering is genuine leather.

Typical features for 1931 are the stainless steel radiator shell with painted inserts, and the stainless steel shell pressed over the bumper escutcheon bolts. The original type Firestone tires can readily be seen.

Photo courtesy Ford Motor Company.

FIGURE 65. 1929 FORD TAXI CAB (135-A).

While some very early Ford catalogs of MODEL A pictured a four door sedan having the characteristic "coupe pillar" and the exposed cowl fuel tank, none were produced except in the form of this Taxi Cab during late 1928 and 1929.

The rear compartment was offset forward on the right to provide space for a "jump seat" for a fourth passenger. The small space remaining to the right of the driver was used for carrying baggage.

Photo courtesy The Henry Ford Museum.

FIGURE 66. 1931 FORD CONVERTIBLE SEDAN — TOP UP.

This smart looking model 400-A, with top in place, appears in a contemporary setting. As with all the MODEL A sport models, the accessories and bright work are either stainless steel or chromium plated. Color of this car is Washington blue with Tacoma cream reveals, trim and wheels. The Goodyear tires are prominent in this photograph.

Neither the Convertible Sedan nor the De Luxe Phaeton were factory equipped with twin side mounted spare wheels except on special order; only *one* was furnished and on the left side. *(See Fig. 67.)*

Photo courtesy Research and Information Dept., Ford Motor Company.

FIGURE 67. 1931 FORD CONVERTIBLE SEDAN — TOP DOWN

The Convertible Sedan is highly prized by collectors today and was quite popular in its day despite its limited production of only 5,085 units. This photograph, dated May 5, 1931, shows the actual pilot model with its top down and boot in place. All upholstering is genuine leather, dark tan in color.

Actual production of this 400-A body style did not begin until May 22. Standard colors were copra drab, Washington blue and Brewster green with contrasting trim and wheels. Note the Firestone tires on this car, and the one-piece splash apron.

Photo courtesy The Henry Ford Museum.

FIGURE 68. 1928 FORD OPEN CAB PICK-UP (Roadster Pickup).

Owned and restored by the Henry Ford Museum in the Armington & Sims shop in the Greenfield Village, this beautiful little 76-A truck continues in daily service throughout the village. Absence of outside door handles and the presence of the small, chamfered-edge brake drums identifies this as a very early MODEL A. It has the hand brake on the left side and has no separate parking brake system.

Features peculiar to all "commercial" Fords are the black painted head lamp and radiator shells, and the pressed steel running boards. On these models the body was green, fenders, wheels and running gear were black.

Photo courtesy Ford Motor Company.

FIGURE 69. 1930 CLOSED CAB PICK-UP — MODEL 82-B.

Ford produced many such "light commercial" cars in various body types on the standard passenger chassis. All had black painted radiator and head lamp shells and black pressed steel running boards, except for one "de luxe" panel delivery truck which was finished bright and with diamond-pattern rubber-covered running boards. Body color is Blue Rock green.

There was a heavier line of trucks rated at 1½ tons and designated as the "AA" Fords. While these larger trucks had lateral rear springs, they were of the cantilever type which served to keep their own weight "spung" the same as with the transverse spring.

Photo by Thomas Shannahan, ANTIQUE AUTOMOBILE Photographer.

FIGURE 70. 1929 FORD TOWN SEDAN.

The author is pictured in his 1929 Ford Town Sedan, 155-A, which was National Second Prize winner at the AACA Lake Forest Meet in 1958. This MODEL A No. A2029467 is fitted with a Murray body No. M601-23938 and has all the extra deluxe features which made the Town Sedan most expensive of the 1929 Ford line.

The external features include nickeled cowl lamps, twin side mounted spare wheels, a fixed trunk with fabric cover, a full length bumper on the rear, a fuel tank *concealed* under the larger cowl, a larger engine hood with the belt line extended forward to the nickeled radiator shell. The FORD Motometer on the radiator cap divulged water temperature.

Interior features were the side and center arm rests, a drop-center floor, assist cords on the rear quarter window posts, robe rail, and plaited Mohair upholstering.

This car is authentically finished in Brewster green lower body, black upper body, black fenders, wheels and running gear. Tires are the original type Firestones.

CHAPTER IX
HELPFUL HINTS

There have been thousands of "tinkerers" who, through the years, have learned many little tricks or "gimmicks" which made life with MODEL A even easier. We can never hope to record even most of these, but we can present a few of the simpler ones most likely to be helpful today:

Always *remove* the dip stick when pouring oil in the engine to vent the crankcase and so prevent "burping" oil out the fill pipe.

Always start the MODEL A engine with the spark lever retarded; otherwise it will kick back and break or bend the starter mechanism (which may be your own arm if you're cranking it!). If you are ever confused about which is "retard" position just remember that TO START UP you must push both levers UP. Then pull the throttle down a few notches, open the choke rod at least a quarter turn to the left, pull the rod out, then step on the starter. As soon as the engine fires, release the choke.

As the engine warms up, lean the carburetor mixture by turning the choke rod to the right—never turn this rod down *tightly* for you will then score and damage the needle valve.

Also retard the spark when the MODEL A is running slowly in high gear, particularly when pulling slowly up a hill.

When installing a new hub cap on any MODEL A wheel, crimp over only four of the tabs, 90° apart. These are enough to hold the cap securely and the unbent tabs will thus be saved for future use. Also be sure to position the hub cap just as it was done in the factory; the FORD script must be able to read upright and horizontal when the wheel is mounted on the spare wheel rack with the valve stem at the *top* position. Always mount the spare wheel on the rack in this position, too.

Keep the "U" bolts tight on both front and rear springs to prevent cracking the cross-members of the frame. When you have occasion to replace a spring, be sure to install a thin resilient cushion, such as leather or rubber-impregnated fabric, between the spring and the cross-member.

Keep center bolts tight in the springs. If a center bolt becomes loose, it may wear and break and allow some leaves or even the entire spring to shift. A rear spring center bolt can be replaced by cutting open a little flap in the sheet steel floor over the spring center, then driving out the bolt and realigning the spring leaves with a tapered drift pin.

Worn horn motor brushes on MODEL A can be replaced with a modern Auto-Lite brush number EW-12 after removing an attached wire from each brush.

To replace either rear axle, or to repair the differential, it is not necessary to remove the entire assembly. Disconnect left brake rod and radius rod; put a block between left spring and axle housing (use a spring spreader if you have one); jack up the chassis on both sides. Remove both rear drums; remove left spring shackle; remove left axle housing from the differential drum; withdraw axle and differential assembly for repair. Replace in reverse order. This job can be done in three hours.

When removing the radiator always unbolt the water inlet and outlet nozzle castings from the engine block and head; it will not be necessary then to touch the hose connections. The radiator shell may remain fastened to the core for this operation.

For removing or installing a MODEL A engine, make up a special eye-bolt by removing the porcelain and electrodes from an old spark plug and then fastening a forged eyebolt through the plug. Screw this into the third spark plug hole for best balance for lifting the engine with a chain hoist or block and tackle.

If you can't find a MODEL A crankshaft ratchet, use one from a Ford V-8—it's better material anyway!

Transmission oil is recommended for use in the MODEL A steering sector housing but this always leaks out. An improved sealing method was used in the 1933 and later Fords and can easily be adapted to the MODEL A steering gear case. Use Part No. 40-3597, steering gear oil retainer tube and plate assembly with gasket No. 40-3592. If you can't find these parts, make the oil seal by silver-soldering a brass tube 6½" long by ½" outside diameter onto the MODEL A Part No. A-3568 plate, keeping it square as shown in the accompanying sketch. Then cut a gasket to match the plate. When installed, the gasket seals the oil in the bottom of the housing and the tube extends through the housing to a point well above the oil level. The original MODEL A seal was merely a thick cork gasket ring which was compressed between the light switch, the switch shaft, and the housing; it is not used in the modification described.

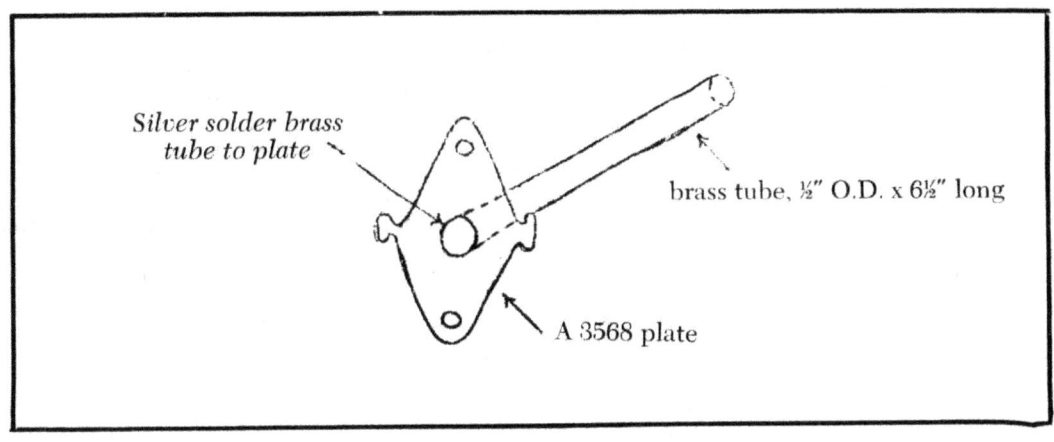

For a quick method of replacing MODEL A distributor points, do not remove the cam and plate from the body, but cut the loop of the spring on the old point arm and remove it, leaving the old bolt in place. Then cut or grind a notch in the outside of the loop of the spring on the new point arm; then just slip the new arm and spring in place over the old bolt. The spring tension will hold it in place. This saves retiming the cam and you won't run the risk of shorting out the wire under the plate, as so often happens when replacing a plate in the distributor body. Actually, the engine *should* be retimed after new points are installed, but this method is sure to save you time and trouble should you have to replace points when on a tour.

Sometimes, if the distributor bushings are badly worn and the shaft is loose, you'll have to set more gap in the points or you will have a miss on one cylinder. Of course the proper way to correct this is to rebush and install a new shaft, but this stop-gap trick will keep you going on all four until you can do a proper job.

Do *not* use a one-piece distributor shaft, if you can help it, when rebuilding the MODEL A distributor assembly. The original two-piece shaft acts as a flexible coupling between the worm gear drive and the distributor body; it is impossible to locate the cylinder head, which supports the distributor body, accurately with respect to the engine block because of the necessary stud hole clearance in the head. If the rigid, one-piece shaft is used, rapid wear of the distributor bearings and run-out of the distributor cam will result.

For best timing of the MODEL A ignition, set breaker points at .020" (range is .018" to .022"). Remove the timing pin from the front of the timing gear cover, reverse it, and insert it in the bolt hole. Turn engine slowly until the pin enters the recess in the cam gear. Number one piston is now on top dead center. *Now* replace timing pin bolt. Retard spark lever. Loosen cam in the distributor and rotate it to the number one electrode in the distributor cap. Then adjust position of cam until the points are just ready to open (the distributor shaft rotates counter clockwise). Tighten cam screw. Turn ignition on and, while slowly advancing the spark lever, listen for a click of sparking at the points, at which time the ammeter will immediately show a slight discharge—about 1½ amperes. The spark lever now should have moved down two notches, or ⅛ inch. Recheck; if lever moves more than two notches, advance the cam slightly by turning counter-clockwise. Tighten cam screw securely; then make a final check.

Accurate results in engine timing are impossible if parts are worn and there is excessive backlash. If you can't immediately replace worn parts, then try to set the cam on the distributor so that, after timing is set as described, the excess movement is in a clockwise direction so that the motion of the drive gear will not have to take up the excess motion before turning the cam end of the distributor shaft. If the backlash is taken up in a counter-clockwise direction, this will have the effect of retarding the spark.

To facilitate accurate adjustment of the distributor timing, make a cam wrench of 1" x ⅛" x 6" long flat steel with an ¹¹⁄₁₆" hole having a ³⁄₁₆" internal stud projecting ¹⁄₃₂". This will fit over the cam and the internal stud will fit into the cam notch to keep it from turning in the wrench. With this wrench the distributor cam can be turned to the desired spot, and *held accurately*, while the cam screw is being tightened.

Under no circumstances should you attempt to adjust the service brakes by turning up the clevises on the brake rods; this would result in the brakes being thrown out of adjustment and cause unequal wear on the linings.

Use chassis lubricant in the MODEL A water pump fittings; the usual "water pump lubricant" will remain solid, and surplus lubricant forced into the cooling system may lodge in the radiator tubes and cause engine overheating. The ordinary chassis lubricant will melt at running temperatures and so cause no radiator blockage.

To overcome excessive end play in the MODEL A water pump shaft, build up the impeller end of the shaft by brazing and grinding or filing the end flat until the factory specified clearing of .006" to .010" is obtained. Excessive clearance results from wear of the shaft end, and wear of the machined thrust boss in the engine head.

Be careful to avoid interchanging the MODEL A fuel tank and radiator caps. While the outward appearance of these is the same, the inside construction is different. The fuel tank cap has a vent hole in the raised portion which allows air to flow from the six tiny openings around the lower edge of the cap. This prevents a vacuum from forming in the fuel tank and stopping flow of gasoline. If a fuel tank cap is used on the radiator it can allow water to leak out. In an emergency, a radiator cap can be used on the fuel tank if it is drilled, but rain water dripping from the windshield visor will leak into the fuel tank through such a vent hole.

When parking MODEL A for any length of time be sure to close the shut-off valve under the fuel tank. Do *not* depend on the carburetor float needle-valve as a positive shut-off, for the entire contents of the fuel tank can leak out through the carburetor valve and create a real fire hazard.

Any inaccuracy of the fuel gage can be corrected by bending the float wire. It is not necessary to remove the gage from the tank to do this if you use two easily made tools. Secure two old MODEL A brake rods and saw off ten inches of the ends with the fixed eye; then cut a ⁵⁄₃₂" gap in the side of each eye. Remove the safety screen from the fuel tank and, reaching through the fill hole, hold the float wire with one eye rod while you bend the wire in the correct direction with the other eye rod.

Always replace the *safety screen* in the fill hole of the fuel tank—this is not merely a strainer but is a safety device to prevent explosion of the fuel tank in the event of a fire at the fill hole.

When shutting off the engine of the 1928 and 1929 MODEL A Fords having the Electrolock "pop-out" ignition switches, press the button all the way in, *but* be sure the "pop-out" button *remains* in! Sometimes, if not pressed firmly, it can pop out again when you stop pressing and after the engine stops turning; this turns the ignition on again and not only can run the battery down but can burn out the high tension coil.

When installing a MODEL A battery, be sure the *positive* pole is grounded. The ammeter will indicate reversed polarity by operating in reverse. Damage to the electrical system and battery can result from reversing polarity of the battery ground.

A knocking noise in the MODEL A engine comes from a worn camshaft timing gear; this also gives poor engine performance. The condition can usually be corrected by installing a new *oversized* (.003" or .004", see parts list) timing gear which compensates for wear on the crankshaft gear.

Breakage of the cam shaft thrust-plunger spring can cause the MODEL A engine to "buck" at low speed. A modern replacement spring which is an exact fit is the Dodge #119996 oil relief valve spring, available from Dodge dealers.

If you notice an annoying vibration in your MODEL A after installing an engine, check the center bolt on the front engine mount. If it is drawn down too tightly it will transmit engine vibration instead of allowing the springs to damp the vibration.

Rubber blocks, or thick rubber washers, can be substituted for the springs in the front engine mount.

After adjusting the MODEL A shock absorber action, it is helpful to install curved pieces of sheet metal on the arm bolt to cover the shock absorber adjusting nut. This deflector permits the brake rod to move up and down past the shock absorber without catching on the nut and bending (SEE SKETCH).

When restoring a MODEL A engine remember that the distributor body and carburetor body were painted black, but all the control levers, rods, springs, sleeves, etc. were *cadmium plated*, not nickeled or chromium plated. The same is true of the wheel lug nuts.

The two fuel lines, tank-to-dash and dash-to-carburetor, were originally made by double lap-rolling sheet brass then *tinning* them to seal them. If either of these tubes is subsequently bent the lapping will separate and the tube will leak. Authentic-looking reproductions can be made of copper or brass tubing—then have them dull tinned or even cadmium plated.

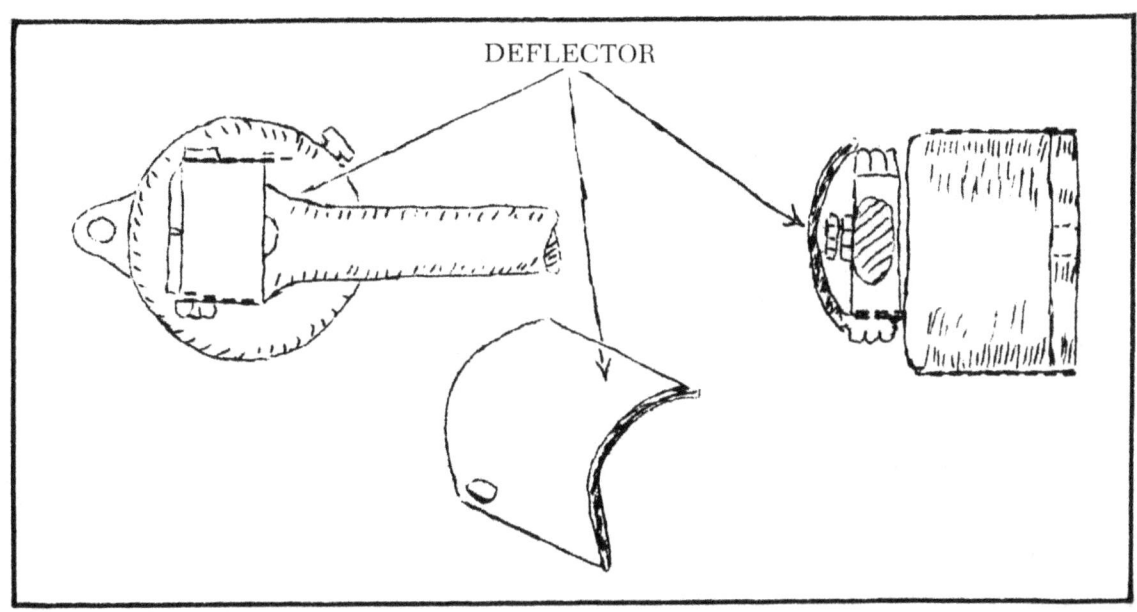

If a spoke of the steering wheel on your MODEL A obscures your view of the speedometer, remove the horn and light switch rod (these need not be pulled all way out for this operation), pull the wheel off the shaft, then reposition it on the shaft. With the 1928-29 wheels there is a choice of several positions because the hub is splined; with the 1930-31 wheels there is a choice of only two keyway positions.

When refastening the light switch assembly at the bottom of the steering column you will have trouble, if working alone, in keeping the switch rod down in place. Spring a light piece of wood, similar to a lath, under the steering wheel and over the light switch lever to hold it down.

When you have occasion to remove the spark and throttle levers from their rods on the steering column tube do not try to drive out the little retaining pins, but shear them off. Use a socket or similar tool which will clear the control rod and which will bear against the lever hub. With someone to hold the control rod down, strike the tool sharply with a hammer to shear the pin. The levers can then be slipped off and new pins installed when the levers are replaced.

Similarly, when removing fenders or other parts held together by fairly small (¼" to ⅜") bolts do not try to turn the nuts off and salvage the bolts, particularly if they are rusted or gummed with road tar. Just shear the bolts off by *tightening* them until they break—this is easier than you may think! It will be easier to reassemble parts with new bolts and nuts anyway.

Frequently it is less expensive to have an old MODEL A radiator recored than to buy one of the current new reproductions. The original water tanks not only preserve the Ford name and authenticity but are much stronger than the new reproductions. The new cores are superior in cooling capacity to the original cores because the tubes are oval in shape rather than circular—this is a detail hard to detect without careful scrutiny.

When having the "bright" parts of your MODEL A replated, remember that for 1928 and 1929 these parts were *nickel* plated and for 1930 and 1931 they were *chromium* plated—there is a big difference! Remember, too, that the larger instrument panel used in the 1928, 1929, and early 1930 MODEL A Fords was *nickel* plated in what is known as "satin finish" to prevent a mirror-like glare from the dash light that would occur with a "bright finish."

To obtain that like-new appearance on road-stained black sidewall tires, daub them with the paste-type black shoe polish, then rub them briskly with a cloth to blend in the polish and remove the excess. The shoe polish dries immediately and does not rub off. This is more convenient than painting tires with the usual black rubber preparation for any shoe polish which gets on even light colored wheels will wipe right off.

Seven different types of springs were used in the MODEL A pasenger car or 103½ chassis. Front springs were all of 10-leaf design (Part No. A5310A), except that a 12-leaf spring (A5310B) was available as special equipment. There were five different types of rear springs, and the style body used on the chassis determined which type was used. These varied, both in the number of leaves as well as the pounds deflection per inch. Below is listed the part numbers, number of leaves and bodies under which each rear spring was used.

A5560A—10 leaves—Tudor, Town Car De Luxe, and Town Car.

A5560—8 leaves—Phaeton, De Luxe Phaeton, Coupe, Sport Coupe and Victoria.

A5560—7 leaves—Roadster.

A5560D—10 leaves—Town Sedan, Fordors De Luxe, Delivery, Special Delivery.

A5560E—10 leaves—Panel Delivery, Pick-up, Station Wagon, Open-Cab and Closed Cab.

The A5560A, A5560D and A5560E all have 10 leaves. To distinguish the latter two apart, the suffix letter "D" or "E" respectively, were stamped on top of one of the spring's leaf clamps. No letter would indicate that the spring was part number A5560A.

The roadster rear spring recquired a dummy leaf (A5585) to take up the additional space left by reason of its having only seven leaves.

In production, the spring leaves were painted with a graphite oil during assembly. After assembly, the springs were spray-painted black.

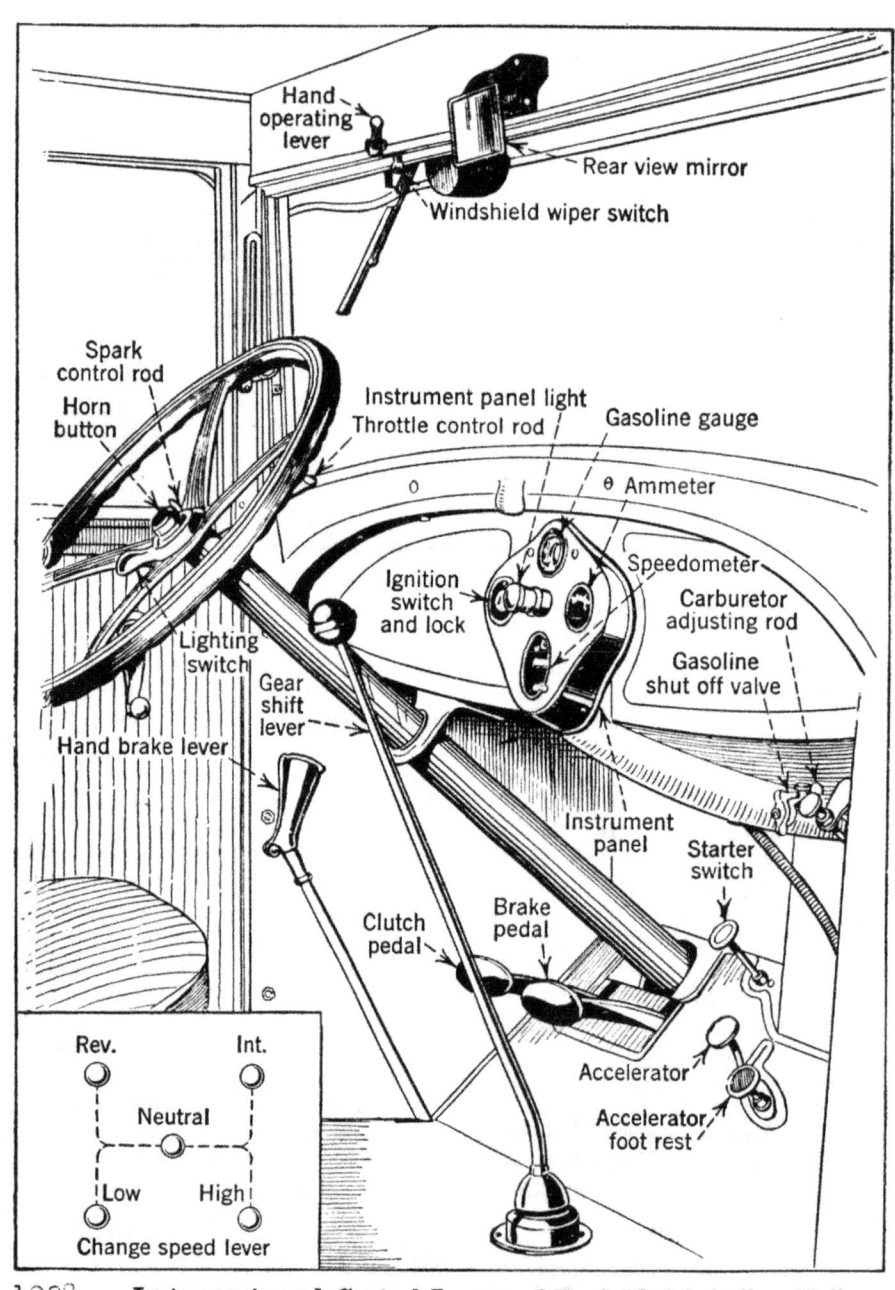

1928 — Instruments and Control Levers of Ford Model A Cars Follow Conventional Practice. Inset Shows Standard Gear Shift Lever Positions.

FIGURE 76. CONTROL ROOM – 1928 FORD.

Photo by Kenneth Stauffer, AACA Photographer.

FIGURE 71. HERSHEY — THE MECCA OF ANCIENT AUTOS.

MODEL A Fords now figure prominently in national "meets" of the AACA such as this huge gathering for two days of fun, picnicking, and contests in the stadium at Hershey, Pa., in 1958.

Of the more than 700 antique cars here, 60 are the MODEL A Fords assembled in the center foreground, and 100 are the Model T Fords surrounding the track. Here all the cars are grouped in official classes according to age and mechanical features for competition and for national recognition for their authenticity and quality of restoration. Both AACA and VMCCA have adopted the same system of car classification. (See also Fig. 41.)

Photo by Kenneth Stauffer, AACA Photographer.

FIGURE 72. LIKE NEW AGAIN!   1929 FORD ROADSTER
Owned and restored by Wendell F. Chapelle, Rathbone, N.Y.

This Roadster, 40-A, with side mounted spare wheel, has the folding trunk rack over the rear bumper; colors are blue body, black fenders, and cream wheels. Upholstering is blue grained.

During many years in storage this car had been vandalized and so severely damaged as to discourage its restoration by anyone but a real MODEL A enthusiast such as Wendell. Since its restoration it took first place in the 1957 MARC Meet at Ford's Greenfield Village and is twice a National First Prize winner in AACA at Pottstown in 1957 and Hershey in 1958.

Note the engine hood held open by the little curved clip on top of the water tank. The side curtains are fine for wet weather—unless you are riding in the rumble seat!

Photo by Kenneth Stauffer, AACA Photographer.

FIGURE 73. THE 1928 ENGINE ROOM.   1928 FORD PHAETON #A650684
Owned and restored by Leslie R. Henry.

Three distinctive features of the 1928 "engine room" visible here are the short, fat "powerhouse" generator, the sheet metal fan shroud on the radiator, and the oblong handle of the oil dipstick. The oil breather pipe extension is an accessory of the period, while the loom-covered generator wire is a genuine Ford replacement for the original steel tube sheath which was an electrical safety hazard.

Since the 1928 headlamps had only one bulb (21-3 C.P.) and only two wires, the metallic tube was only ½" in diameter and the hole in the radiator shell was 13/16". These sizes were changed to 9/16" and 15/16" in 1929 for all cars not equipped with cowl lamps.

FIGURE 74. THE 1929 ENGINE ROOM   1929 FORD PHAETON #2029467
Owned and restored by Leslie R. Henry.

Characteristic of the 1929 (and later) MODEL A "engine rooms" are the longer, conventional type generator, the glass bowl fuel strainer, and the little, round handle of the oil dipstick. Visible is the steering column typical of the 7-tooth, non-adjustable steering gear.

The bolted center panel of the firewall is distinctive of the town sedan and the Fordor sedan; removal of this panel permits the fuel tank to be dropped free of the separate body cowl.

Since the town sedan was factory equipped with cowl lamps, the head lamps have only one bulb (21-21 C.P.) and only two wires in the smaller ½" metallic tubes through the radiator shell. There is no fan shroud on the radiator.

Photo by Kenneth Stauffer, AACA Photographer.

FIGURE 75. CONTROL ROOM — 1928 FORD.

Here appear some of the characteristics of the late 1928 Fords; the longer choke rod which extends past the fuel tank instead of being entirely underneath; the hand brake lever which is the hand-squeeze type but which has been moved from the left side to a position in front of the shift lever. The 1929 and later Fords had the brake lever placed to the right of the shift lever, operated by a thumb-press button.

The nickel-plated instrument panel is identical for all 1928, 1929 and 1930 Fords; this panel was plated with a *satin finish* nickel to avoid any glare from the dash light.

Notice the rubber-capped foot rest button to the right of the accelerator pedal— this was a must in those days of rough roads so the driver could hold his foot steady on the accelerator! In 1928 the electric windshield wiper and wind wings were not yet factory equipment for any open-body Fords, but were added by dealers or owners after delivery.

The car pictured here is a late 1928 Ford Phaeton #A650684 owned and restored by the author.

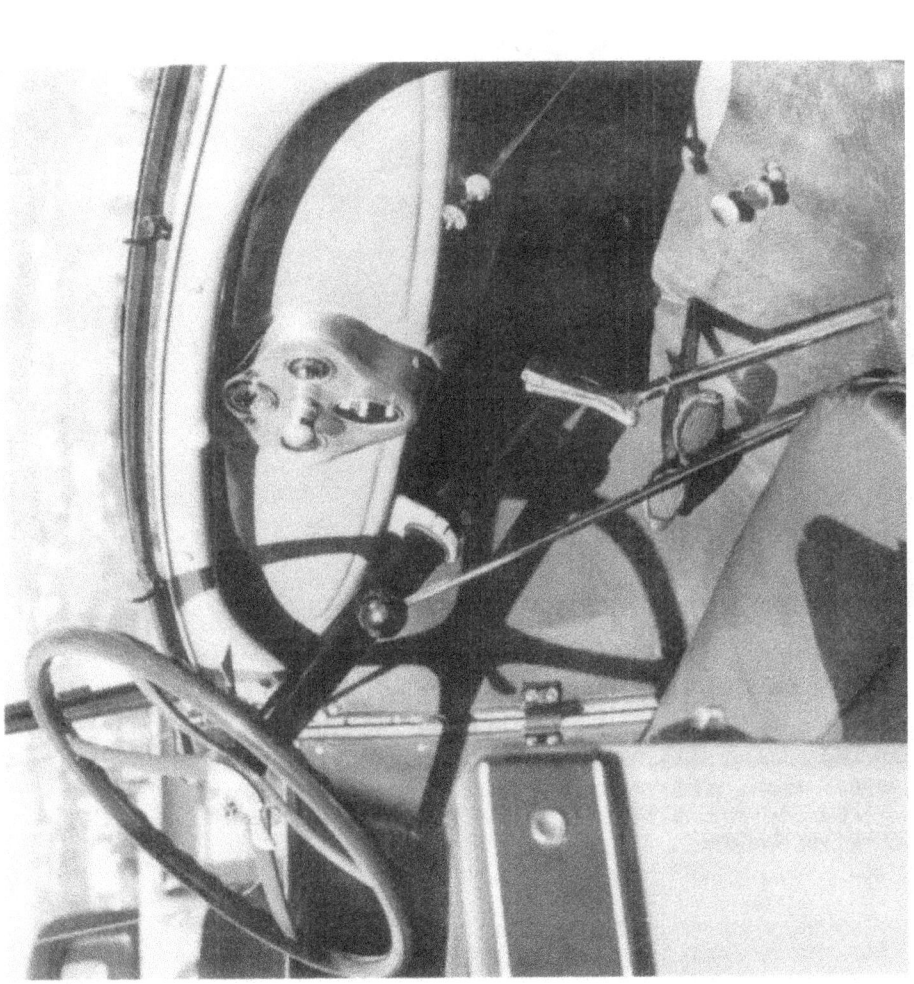

Photo courtesy Ford Motor Company.

FIGURE 77. CONTROL ROOM — 1931 FORD.

In this convertible sedan, 400-A, appear the controls characteristic of all 1931 MODEL A Fords; note the flat steering wheel (compare with Fig. 75), the oval, ribbed instrument panel with round speedometer, the vacuum-powered windshield wiper motor, and the hand brake at the right of shift lever.

In this convertible body, the side rails are rigidly fixed to the body while the tan rubberized fabric snaps along its upper edge to close the top.

Photo courtesy Ford Motor Company.

FIGURE 78.   EARLY 1928 FORDOR SEDAN.

The small, chamfered brake drums and the green celluloid sun visor mark this Fordor as one of the earliest. The Briggs-built body features a seal brown fabric top and rear panel and a cowl ventilator on left side only. This is the first body style to have the smooth, streamlined cowl with a concealed fuel tank.

Photo by Kenneth Stauffer, AACA Photographer.

FIGURE 79.   1931 FORD DE LUXE PHAETON — TOP UP.

Owned by H. Allen Moore, Eagle, Pa., this 1931 two door phaeton was restored in 1958. Except for the radiator shell, this is identical to the 1930 de luxe phaeton, and even bears the same designation, 180-A. While not a competition restoration, this is a fine example of the serious collector's work. Authentic colors are stone brown, Tacoma cream wheels, black fenders and running gear.

CHAPTER X
ENGINE NUMBERS AND ASSEMBLY RECORDS

Contrary to popular belief, MODEL A Fords cannot be reliably dated by their engine numbers. Neither can MODEL A Ford production rates nor volumes be accurately determined by the engine numbers even though these were also the cars' serial numbers.* The serial number was stamped on each engine at the time of its assembly in the Rouge plant, where all engines were built, and not at the assembly plants where the engines were mounted in the car chassis.

"For that reason," says Owen Bombard of the Ford Motor Company Research and Information Department, "there were engines 'in float' to our various assembly plants (45 in number at that time). Even a few hundred engines in transit to each of these assembly plants would give a fairly sizable discrepancy between the number of engines manufactured each month and the number of cars assembled.

"Foreign production was included as a part of the United States engine number series because all engines for foreign-sold MODEL A Fords were built in the United States with the exception of Canadian production and a small number made in Manchester, England. Allowing for this small number of foreign-built engines, there was a surplus of engines over cars produced for each year except 1931:

  1,089 excess engines in 1927.
  60,912 excess engines in 1928.
  69,278 excess engines in 1929.
  79,456 excess engines in 1930.
  138,895 excess CARS in 1931.

The reason there were more cars than engines produced in 1931 is, of course, because the engine inventory float finally caught up with the car assembly orders."

It is difficult to establish the exact date of manufacture, or more properly, assembly, of the 1930 and 1931 Fords, but it is quite easy to date the 1928 and 1929 Fords, for those have the assembly date stamped on the lower left corner of the firewall section of the fuel tank, under the hood.

Included here as helpful to the MODEL A restorer is a list of the MODEL A ENGINE NUMBERS by months, and a list of MODEL A ASSEMBLY RECORD TYPES which shows annual assembly records by body style. This latter information, never before published, may aid in establishing assembly dates when used in conjunction with the ENGINE NUMBER list.

*Each MODEL A engine number was also struck on the top-left frame side member opposite the rear engine support, thus becoming the car serial number. In order to read this number after assembly, the body and fender of all Fords, and the splash apron of the late 1930-31 Fords, must be removed.

UNITED STATES AUTO & TRUCK PRODUCTION
1924 through 1934
Comparisons of FORD with CHEVROLET and with TOTAL U. S. productions.

Year	FORD Production	% of U. S.	CHEVROLET Production	% of U. S.	UNITED STATES Total Production	FORD PROFIT (or Loss)
1924	1,992,000	49.0	314,000	7.7	4,100,000	$100,000,000
1925	1,999,000	45.4	532,000	12.0	4,427,000	$ 80,000,000
1926	1,629,000	36.2	732,000	16.2	4,500,000	$ 75,000,000
1927	843,700*	23.5	1,001,000	28.9	3,583,000	$ 30,280,000
1928	818,700	17.7	1,200,000	26.0	4,631,000	-$ 72,000,000
1929	1,951,000	34.5	1,333,000	23.5	5,651,000	$ 92,000,000
1930	1,485,600	42.5	863,000	24.4	3,509,000	$ 41,700,000
1931**	762,000	30.8	780,000	31.5	2,472,000	-$ 37,000,000
1932	342,000	23.9	411,000	28.6	1,431,000	-$ 70,900,000
1933	411,000	16.6	474,000	18.8	2,625,000	-$ 7,900,000
1934	859,000	29.9	867,000	30.1	2,870,000	$ 23,000,000

 *Production was 839,527 Model T; 4,186 MODEL A—Ford plant shut down June to October.
 **Ford production changed over to include V-8 line; 4-cylinder line not discontinued until September, '32.
 Figures from THE AUTOMOBILE INDUSTRY by E. D. Kennedy, published by Reynal & Hitchcock, New York, 1941; compilation by the author.

MODEL A and AA
ASSEMBLY RECORD TYPES
A condensed table prepared by Leslie R. Henry
from data of Ford Motor Company — Production Department Annual Reports*

		PHAETON	DELUXE PHAETON	ROADSTER	DELUXE ROADSTER	STANDARD COUPE	SPORT COUPE	BUSINESS COUPE	DELUXE COUPE	VICTORIA COUPE	TUDOR SEDAN	DELUXE 2 DOOR SEDAN	STANDARD SEDAN 4 DOOR	FORDOR SEDAN	DELUXE SEDAN
1927 10/21 to 12/31		35-A		40-A		45-A	50-A				55-A				
	Domestic	221	—	251	—	611	732	—	—	—	1798	—	—	—	—
	Foreign	0	—	18	—	18	22	—	—	—	150	—	—	—	—
	Total	221	—	269	—	629	754	—	—	—	1948	—	—	—	—
1928 1/1 to 12/31		35-A		40-A	40-A	45-A	50-A	54-A	—	—	55-A	—	—	60-A	—
	Domestic	47255	—	51807	30130	70784	79099	37343	—	—	203562	—	—	82749	—
	Foreign	20921	—	3607	1955	2811	3026	258	—	—	30773	—	—	6179	—
	Total	68176	—	55504	32085	73595	82125	37601	—	—	234340	—	—	88928	—
1929 1/1 to 12/31		35-A		40-A		45-A	50-A	54-A	—	—	55-A	—	165-A,B 170-A,B	60-A,B,C	—
	Domestic	49813	—	191529	—	178982	134292	57644	—	—	523922	—	53941	146097	—
	Foreign	40473	—	12377	—	5039	4576	933	—	—	25545	—	725	21031	—
	Total	90291	—	203906	—	184021	138868	58577	—	—	549467	—	54666	167128	—
1930 1/1 to 12/31		35-B	130-A	40-B	40-B	45-B	50-B	54-A	45-B	190-A	55-B	—	165-C,D	—	170-B
	Domestic	16470	3946	112901	11313	226027	69167	0	29937	6306	376271	—	41133	—	12854
	Foreign	23416	419	9302	211	6637	3405	110	340	141	48873	—	12825	—	856
	Total	39886	4365	122203	11524	232664	72572	110	29777	6447	425144	—	53958	—	13710
1931 1/1 to 12/31		35-B	130-A	40-B	40-B	45-B	50-B	—	45-B	190-A	55-B	21984	165-C,D	—	170-B
	Domestic	4076	2229	5499	52997	79316	19700	—	23067	33906	148425	21984	13127	—	3251
	Foreign	6984	646	2294	3705	3069	1572	—	586	1924	33220	1506	7593	—	1716
	Total	11060	2875	7793	56702	82385	21272	—	23653	35830	170845	23490	20720	—	4967
1932 1/1 to 4/30		35-B	130-A	40-B	40-B	45-B	50-B	—	45-B	190-A	55-B	—	165-C,D	—	170-B
	Total	309	41	134	4	9	19	—	43	33	105	—	22	—	15

*On file in Ford Archives.

*Ford pioneered **assembly line** production of Station Wagons in the industry in 1929.

**Many of the Commercial Chassis were sent to the several independent builders of Station Wagon bodies; there is no way of knowing how many Station Wagons were thus produced.

***World production of cars & trucks, including Walkerville, Canada and **Manchester, England.**

****United States and Foreign engine production, except engines built in Walkerville and Manchester.

Note that engine numbers were stamped on the blocks as they left the engine assembly line. There was considerable time lag until an engine was finally mounted in a chassis on the car assembly line.

CABRIOLET	SEDAN 2 WINDOW	CONVERTIBLE SEDAN	TOWN SEDAN	TOWN CAR	TAXI CAB	STATION WAGON*	COMMERCIAL CHASSIS**	TRUCKS	ANNUAL PRODUCTION TOTAL	CUMULATIVE PRODUCTION TOTAL***	MOTOR NUMBERS**** (PUBLISHED BY FORD CO. 1955)
---	---	---	---	---	---	---	99	286	3993	3993	1
---	---	---	---	---	---	---	0	0	133	133	to
---	---	---	---	---	---	---	99	286	4186	4186	5275
											5275
				140–A	135–A	150–A					5276
---	---	---	---	89	264	5	42607	63231	713523	717521	to
---	---	---	---	0	0	0	18463	17121	105211	105399	810122
---	---	---	---	39	264	5	61070	80352	818734	822920	804847
68–A		155–A,B	140–A	135–A	150–A						810123
16421	---	34970	913	4576	4954	130603	58277	1704945	2422466	to
1343	---	6203	100	281	0	27684	17121	246147	351546	2742695
17764	---	41173	1013	4857	4954	158272	75398	1951092	2774012	1932573
63–B		155–C,D	140–B	135–A	150–B						2742696
25368	5279	104935	63	10	3510	56708	152341	1267033	3689499	to
3358	2552	17522	33	263	289	26020	67000	218569	570115	4237500
29226	7831	122534	96	273	3799	82728	220341	1485602	4259614	1494305
68–B,C		155–C,D	140	135–A	150–B						4237501
11801	---	55469	---	0	2843	34959	103561	626559	4316058	to
2105	---	9976	---	7	170	15454	53848	135509	705724	4830306
13706	---	65447	---	7	3013	50413	157409	762068	5021782	593506
68–B,C	400–A	155–C,D									4830307
19	---	139	---	---	---	---	---	905	5022687	to
											4849340

400–A
4864
208
5072

400–A
13

ASSEMBLY RECORD TYPES — JANUARY 1st TO DECEMBER 31st, 1928

BRANCH	PHAE.	ROAD.	ROAD. • RUMBLE SEAT	STD. COUPE	SPORT COUPE	BUSI- NESS COUPE	TUDOR	FORDOR	TOWN CAR	TAXI CAB	COM'L CHASSIS	TRUCK CHASSIS	TOTAL	DUAL HIGH	"A" PANEL BODY	"AA" PANEL BODY	CLOSED CABS	OPEN CABS	STAKE BODY	PLAT- FORM BODY	EX- PRESS BODY	PICK-UP BOX
Atlanta	1587	805	463	1087	1339	697	3460	1568	2	4	718	991	12741	264	72	41	793	556	403	13	81	525
Buffalo	435	1790	144	2295	2009	1257	5183	2194	2	6	1399	1258	17970	571	87	44	1214	665	533	7	74	834
Charlotte	1639	1336	875	2114	1696	939	3550	1753	1	2	734	1017	15656	202	69	41	696	500	368	0	73	513
Chester	826	1471	2566	2968	3125	1757	9001	3283	2	4	1918	2552	29271	512	229	196	2112	839	972	9	226	1008
Chicago	621	2696	1249	3477	4589	2179	14138	5300	11	31	2484	5285	40060	1095	352	198	2894	1138	1629	125	279	1389
Cincinnati	654	747	671	1833	1397	667	2565	1652	2	6	735	614	11513	188	64	36	619	219	201	13	36	372
Cleveland	60	443	218	1146	524	225	1273	791	1	11	340	148	5184	24	27	8	192	71	52		16	113
Columbia	221	936	355	1544	903	440	2690	1548	1	9	465	645	9757	113	72	52	571	308	366	7	57	343
Dallas	1644	1956	702	3046	2767	1428	4588	2748	0	5	1303	1442	21627	261	66	63	1275	828	712	38	103	846
Denver	241	721	2	1099	875	601	2010	1620	1	2	776	811	8759	366	61	59	813	505	340	30	70	648
Des Moines	187	886	174	1378	924	600	4391	1677	1	5	492	913	11628	374	71	52	839	303	64	283	8	339
Houston	1754	1214	658	2162	1868	1161	2556	2563	1	5	1115	1113	15770	406	70	61	1101	845	776		139	903
Indianapolis	298	877	663	1757	1237	603	4290	1597	1	7	681	994	13005	315	91	63	916	334	372	22	8	467
Jacksonville	1223	1521	930	958	1647	996	3570	2033	1	2	814	1493	15192	1150	100	35	850	573	495	45	19	575
Kansas City	1892	4470	658	4632	4151	2052	12640	4397	2	5	1731	2968	40647	1241	133	104	2736	1124	1193	440	220	1317
Kearny	12375	5428	2530	2896	7782	2851	20239	6656	12	10	4928	14024	77734	2957	152	94	4758	2424	2701	11	331	1691
Los Angeles	534	1486	663	2333	2838	1043	2453	3181	6	13	1194	1385	17130	451	104	106	984	807	590	52	144	786
Louisville	2750	3059	1574	2577	5564	1568	8667	2406	2	14	1281	2101	29355	590	107	57	1816	691	897	8	91	746
Memphis	2906	2186	879	2254	2172	1271	5616	2505	1	7	967	1285	22049	244	73	51	1149	616	488		46	729
Milwaukee	195	826	229	1869	1295	619	3669	2278	1	12	868	869	12750	414	80	40	858	440	271		50	583
New Orleans	1662	1049	606	1442	1546	905	2591	1782	1	5	842	975	15406	203	87	50	731	505	345	3	44	516
Norfolk	3164	2559	1405	3151	3306	1131	7066	2432	3	5	1596	2000	27818	581	176	79	1575	1050	968	3	277	1009
Oklahoma City	935	1820	701	3455	2312	1424	3666	2430	1	1	1020	1525	19288	568	90	72	1412	720	762	89	148	715
Omaha	250	882	190	1794	1194	910	4609	2229	1	6	576	1014	13655	621	69	56	1015	309	103	434	44	391
Pittsburgh	357	921	792	2305	1449	813	2879	1477	2	16	802	878	12691	273	64	59	895	527	299	9	220	531
Portland	118	351	34	472	167	73	689	603	1	1	219	268	2995	107	60	29	228	140	44	9	16	159
St. Louis	1682	2199	549	2678	3000	1547	8102	2405	1	13	1590	1887	25653	492	138	115	1670	782	550	91	87	951
San Francisco	807	1124	568	1479	3007	1073	4978	2111	1	4	1313	1335	17800	295	66	55	1172	773	526	34	231	862
Seattle	401	855	145	1062	1337	755	2968	1821	1	3	972	890	11210	512	70	27	745	566	237	20	84	569
Somerville	915	1065	1362	2578	2587	1313	8339	3047	4	15	2254	2034	25513	413	195	121	1748	938	752	32	150	1053
Twin City	579	1930	412	2669	2307	1645	12143	5169	5	16	1877	2777	31529	1034	239	103	2897	907	574	908	95	1582
Rouge	4377	4198	6298	4274	10187	2996	34183	5293	18	17	4608*	7738	84187	1764	420	341	5978	5169	3117	86	670	3206
DOMESTIC TOTAL	47255	51807	30130	70784	79099	37343	208562	82349	89	264	42612	63229	715525	18583	3744	2486	47212	23972	21680	2781	4087	26171
Antwerp	424	8	60	28	50	31	2008	187			58	868	3702									
Amieres	245	3	9	16	3	83	403	103			163	86	1116									
Barcelona	579	12	33	48	123	14	1235	238			20	928	3230									
Berlin	200	20	47	36	29	21	1078	234			50	778	2543									
Buenos Aires	200	38	78	48	65	25	500	130			116	1200	4200									
Copenhagen	851	5	12	29	47	10	2188	565			194	1379	5055									
Mexico City	525	6	18	36	29	9	102	106			2	265	1079									
Sao Paulo	1033	18	45	17		4	29	41			107	602	1895									
Yokohama	927			8		7	97	5			140	674	1847									
DETROIT TOTAL	54039	51915	30432	71021	79435	37544	216172	83808	89	264	43462	70009	738190									454401
Manchester	288	46	138	108	200	57	2008	433			748	1579	5746									93972
GRAND TOTAL	54327	51961	30570	71129	79635	37601	218521	84241	89	264	44210	71588	745936									548620
Walkerville	13848	3543	1515	2466	2490		21019	4297			16865	8764	74798									
TOTAL FORD "A"	64175	55504	32085	73595	82125	37601	239540	88538	89	264	61075	80352	818734									

Complete units shipped to Export

	Model T	Model A
Assembly Plants	529164	188
Rouge Assembly	18577	3998
Foreign Assembly	65361	0
Walkerville	37515	
TOTALS	650415	4186
Tractors		
Lincoln		

Lincoln	6330
Tractors	8001
TOTAL UNITS	835065
	66795

Of Rouge commercial chassis five were assembled into Station Wagons and two into Ambulances.

FIGURE 96. THE FORD MOTOR COMPANY PRODUCTION DEPARTMENT ANNUAL REPORT FOR 1928.

Shown here are the numbers of each type MODEL A Ford produced during 1928 at each of the domestic and foreign assembly plants. Manchester, England and Walkerville, Canada are listed separately because these were complete factories and had their own series of engine numbers, which were also the Ford automobile serial numbers.

Reproduced by courtesy Ford Motor Company Archives.

Model A Motor Numbers

Month	First No.	Last No.
1927		
October 20, 1927	1	137
November	138	971
December	972	5275
1928		
January	5276	17251
February	17252	36016
March	36017	67700
April	67701	109740
May	109741	165726
June	165727	224276
July	224277	295707
August	295708	384867
September	384868	473012
October	473013	585696
November	585697	697829
December	697830	810122
1929		
January	810123	983136
February	983137	1127171
March	1127172	1298827
April	1298828	1478647
May	1478648	1663401
June	1663402	1854831
July	1854832	2045422
August	2045423	2243920
September	2243921	2396932
October	2936933	2571781
November	2571782	2678140
December	2678141	2742695

Model A Motor Numbers (Continued)

Month	First No.	Last No.
1930		
January	2742696	2826649
February	2826650	2940776
March	2940777	3114465
April	3114466	3304703
May	3304704	3509306
June	3509307	3702547
July	3702548	3771362
August	3771363	3883888
September	3883889	4005973
October	4005974	4093995
November	4093996	4177733
December	4177734	4237500
1931		
January	4237501	4310300
February	4310301	4393627
March	4393628	4520831
April	4520832	4611921
May	4611922	4695999
June	4696000	4746730
July	4746731	4777282
August	—	—
September	4777283	4824809
October	4824810	4826746
November	4826747	4830806
December	—	—
1932		
January	4830807	4842983
February	4842984	4846691
March	4846692	4849340

Photo courtesy Research and Information Dept., Ford Motor Company.

FIGURE 80. 1931 FORD DE LUXE ROADSTER.

This Ford Motor Company photo shows a 1931 de. luxe roadster, 40-B, just as it came off the Rouge assembly line. The folding trunk rack, visible on the back, was one of the many "regular" accessories supplied with the car; the white side wall tires (Firestone) were extra. It should be noted that *only* the de luxe roadsters were factory equipped with twin side mounted spare wheels as "regular" items. All other Model A Fords with twin spare wheels had them so equipped on special order or by the dealer after delivery.

Photo by Kenneth Stauffer, AACA Photographer.

FIGURE 81. ROADSTERS ARE MOST POPULAR TODAY.

Clarence Hartley, Jr., of York, Pennsylvania, is the envy of many a collector with this beautiful 1931 Ford de luxe roadster 40-B he restored. In addition to its popular appeal, this car was judged National First Prize winner at the AACA Hershey (Pa.) Meet in 1957.

Popular also is its color combination, Washington blue and Tacoma cream body and wheels, with tan leather front seat. The rumble seat, shown open, is a matching tan leatherette.

FIGURE 82. SOMETIMES EVEN MODEL A BROKE DOWN!

Continual pulling through the sands of Cape May Point, New Jersey, finally incapacitated this 1928 Roadster in 1931, the owner overhauled it right where it stopped on the beach, just above high tide!

Photo courtesy Ford Motor Company.

FIGURE 83. 1929 STANDARD PHAETON.

The phaetons were quite popular with police departments and the armed forces. Though normally furnished with semi-gloss black grained top material, this phaeton (35-A) was fitted with a khaki top for United States Army "official use only". Note the spare wheel mounted with the valve stem at the top.

Photo courtesy The Henry Ford Museum.

FIGURE 84. FUN WITH FORDS.

Field events and judging for quality and authenticity of restoration are part of the program of this Model A Restorer's Club meet held near the "Secretary House" in the Greenfield Village, Dearborn, Michigan. In the foreground is the early 1928 Ford roadster pickup truck belonging to the Henry Ford Museum, host to the MARC for this annual meet. (See also Fig. 25.)

FIGURE 85. DUNE RUNNING — A MODERN SPORT FOR OLD CARS.

Soft, shifting sand holds no terror for these "dune" or "beach buggies." Here stripped-down MODEL A Fords are easily a match for the younger V-8s and Jeeps as they cavort on 8.20 x 15 tires with 5 pounds of air pressure. The two-wheel drive MODEL A pulls out of extra soft spots in which a four-wheel drive car would simply bury itself.

CHAPTER XI
SPECIFICATIONS AND RESTORATION DATA

AXLE, FRONT
Material — Chrome aloy forging.
Caster — 5°
Type — "I" section; reverse Elliott.
Bearings — Taper roller, adjustable.
  Inner Cup — Bower #A-1202. Inner Cone — Timken #A-1201. Outer Cup — Bower #A-1217. Outer Cone — Timken #A-1216.

AXLE, REAR
Material — Ford carbon manganese steel.
Type — Three-quarter floating.
Bearings — Straight roller.
Gear type — Spiral bevel gear.
Gear ratio — 3.70 to 1 (3.77 & 4.11 optional).
Ring gear — 8.4" pitch diameter.
Shaft — 1⅛" diameter.
Pinion bearing — Double taper roller.
Differential bearings — Single taper roller.
Differential gears — Integral with axles.

BATTERY
Type — Ford
Ground — Positive pole ground.
Capacity — 80 ampere-hours; 3 cells; 39 plates.
Charging rate — 10 to 12 amperes.

BRAKES
Service
Type — Ford; mechanical, internal expanding.
Foot pedal — Four-wheels.
Adjustment — Square stud outside operating a wedge.
Percent of braking power —
  Front wheels 40.
  Rear wheels 60.
Brake shoe lining — Woven wire asbestos, 14" long x 1½" wide x 3/16" thick; two shoes per wheel.
Brake drum — 11" diameter x 1¾" wide.
Total braking surface — 168 sq. in.

Parking
Type — Rear brake shoes pick-up.
Hand lever — Located on left frame rail; hand grip release.
Adjustment — Screwed clevis on linkage plus screw wedge.
Brake shoe lining —
Brake drum —
Total braking surface — 84 sq. in.

CAMSHAFT
Diameter — ⅞"
Bearings —
  Five, each 1-9/16" in diameter
  Length front — 1¾"
  Length second — ⅞"
  Length third — 2"
  Length fourth — ⅞"
  Length fifth — 1"
Cam lift — .302"
Cam gear — Bakelized material; 50 spiral cut teeth.

CARBURETOR
Make — Zenith
Material — Cast iron
Adjustment — Manual by rotating choke rod under dash panel.

CLUTCH
Type — Ford, multiple disc, dry.
Number of discs — 4 driving, 5 driven.

CONNECTING ROD
Material — Steel forging, "X" section
  (Also some welded tubular section).
Length — 7½"
Crank end — Babbitt, 1½" diam. x 1⅝" long
Piston end — Babbitt, 1" diam. x 1⅝" long.

COOLING SYSTEM
Type — Thermo-syphon plus centrifugal pump.
Fan — Two blade "airplane" type, 16" diam.
Drive — ⅝" "V" belt; 1½ times engine speed.
Radiator core — Fin & tube; shrouded for fan.
Radiator shell — Steel, bright nickel finish.
Capacity, system — 3 gallons.
Radiator hose —
  Upper 2" diam. x 6¼" long.
  Lower 1¾" diam. x 2¾" long.

CRANKSHAFT
Material — Ford carbon manganese steel.
Length — 26¼" overall.
Main bearings —
  1⅝" diam. x 2" long, front & center.
  1⅝" diam. x 3" long, rear.
Crank bearings — 1½" diam. x 1⅝" long.
Crank gear — Steel, 25 spiral-cut teeth.

ENGINE
Bore & Stroke — 3⅞" x 4¼".
Horsepower — S.A.E. rating 24.03 H.P.
Horsepower — Brake H.P. 40 at 2200 R.P.M.
Torque — 128 ft. lbs. at 1000 R.P.M.
Displacement — 200.5 cu. in.
Compression Ratio — 4.22 to 1.
Compression — 76 P.S.I., gage.
Firing Order — 1, 2, 4, 3,
Material — Gray iron casting.
Cylinders — 4, cast en bloc; ⅛" offset.
Type — 4 cycle, "L" head, 8 valves on right.
Head — Demountable, held by 12 7/16" studs.
Suspension — 4 point.
Flywheel — Cast iron.
Ring gear — 112 teeth; 14.2" outside diam.
Total Weight — 475 lbs. including clutch & transmission.
Color — Ford Engine Green, Ditzler Co. #DE-40133.

FUEL TANK
Capacity — 11 gallons.

GENERATOR
Type — Ford, "powerhouse"; 6 pole, 5 brush.
Speed — 1½ times engine speed.
Charging Rate — 12 amperes, normal.

IGNITION
Battery — Ford; 6 volts; 80 ampere-hours 39 plates.
Coil — Ford.
Distributor — Ford design eliminating high tension wires to spark plugs.
Breaker Points — Gap .016" to .022".
Spark Plug — ⅞" S.A.E.; Champion No. 3; gap .025 to .030.
Lock — "Electrolock"; theft-proof armored cable to distributor.

LIGHTS
Head Lights
Material — Steel, finished in bright nickel.
Design — Acorn.
Make — Ford.
Lens — Ford; vertical flutes; 8½" diameter.
Bulb — 2 filament; 21 C.P. and 3 C.P.
Tail & Stop Lights
Material — Steel backing plate, brass cover, finished in bright nickel.
Make — Ford "Duolight".
LUBRICATION
Engine
Type — Gear pump to valve chamber; gravity flow to main bearings; splash to other parts.
Oil Capacity — 5 quarts.
Chassis
Type — Alemite pressure grease gun & fittings.
PISTONS
Material — Aluminum.
Length — 3-29/32".
Ring groove width —
  Upper two, ⅛", compression.
  Lower one, 5/32", oil control.
Ring groove depth — 7/32", all.
ROAD CLEARANCE
Road Clearance — 9½" at differential housing.
SHOCK ABSORBERS
Type — Houdaille, double acting, hydraulic.
SPRINGS
Material — Chrome steel.
Type — Transverse.
Front Spring, all cars — 10 leaves; 1¾" wide; 31" free length.
Rear Spring, closed cars — 10 leaves; 2¼" wide; 39" free length.
Rear Spring, open cars — 8 leaves; 2¼" wide; 39½" free length.

STARTING MOTOR
Terminal grounded — Positive.
Normal armature speed — 1500 R.P.M.
Shaft diameter — ½".
Type of drive — Abell.
STEERING GEAR
Type — Worm & 7-tooth sector.
Ratio — 11¼ to 1.
Steering wheel — 17" diameter, red composition.
TIRES
Type — Firestone Balloon, for drop-center rims.
Size — 30 x 4.50 (4.50 x 21).
Pressure — 35 P.S.I., front and rear.
DRIVE
Torque tube.
TRANSMISSION
Type — Selective sliding gear (standard).
Make — Ford.
TREAD
Standard Tread — 56"
TURNING DISTANCE
Radius — 17'
Circle — 34'
VALVES
Arrangement — Vertical, right side.
Material — Carbon chrome nickel.
Lift — .287.
Seat angle — 45°
Spring pressure — 36 lbs.
Stem diameter — 5/16"
Head — Mushroom.
Tappet clearance — .015".
WHEELBASE
Wheelbase — 103½".

Changes Between the 1928 & 1929 Model A Ford

Engine	1928	1929
Suspension	4 points	3 points
Camshaft bearings	5	3
Length front	1¾ in.	1¾ in.
Length second	⅞ in.	Omitted
Length third	2 in.	2 in.
Length fourth	⅞ in.	Omitted
Length fifth	1 in.	1 in.
Valve material	Carbon chrome nickel alloy	Chrome Silicon alloy
Spark plug gap	.015 to .020	.025 to .030

Rear Axle

Gear Ratio	3.7 to 1	3.77 to 1 4.111 to 1 Optional

SOME ABBREVIATIONS USED IN THIS BOOK
AACA — Antique Automobile Club of America.
ALAM — Association of Licensed Automobile Manufacturers
Amp. — Ampere.
Cu. In. — Cubic inch.
HCCA — Horseless Carriage Club of America.
HP — Horse Power.
MAFCA — Model A Ford Club of America.
MARC — Model A Restorer's Club.
MPH — Miles per hour.
psi. — Pounds per square inch, gauge pressure.
SAE — Society of Automotive Engineers.
VMCCA — Veteran Motor Car Club of America.
" — Inch.

LICENSE DATA
License information covering the new Ford cars is given below:
Engine number stamped on left side of cylinder block.
  Number of Cylinders — 4
  Cylinder Bore — 3⅞ in.
  Stroke — 4¼ in.
  Piston Displacement — 200.5 cu. in.
  Horsepower—S.A.E. — 24.03
  Wheelbase — 103½ in.

CLEARANCE LIMITS FOR ASSEMBLY OF "A" ENGINES
(Ford Service Bulletin, June 1931)
(All dimensions in inches)

Piston in cylinders — .002 maximum.
Piston ring gap, lower ring — .008 to .010.
Piston ring gap, center ring — .010 to .012.
Piston ring gap, upper ring — .012 to .015.
Ring groove clearance — .001.
Piston pin fit in connecting rod bushing — .0003 maximum.
Pin in piston — .0002 to .0005 shrink fit.
Pistons assembled with split side toward left side of engine.
Connecting rod side play on crankshaft — .008 to .012.
Connecting rod clearance between piston bosses — .040 to .053.
Connecting rod clearance on crankshaft diameter — .001.
Connecting rods assembled with oil dips toward camshaft.
Crankshaft end play — .002 to .004.
Main bearing clearance — .001.
Camshaft bearing clearance — .003 maximum.
Camshaft end play taken up by tention of spring in front cover. Spring tension approximately 35 lbs.
Valves to push rod clearance — .010 to .013.
Exhaust valves in valve guides — .002.
Intake valves in valve guides — .001 to .0015.
Valve lift — .287.
Push rod clearance — .0015.
Timing gear backlash — .004.
End play of water pump shaft — .006 to .010.
Flywheel eccentricity and wobble (indicator reading) after mounting on crankshaft, not more than .005.
Breaker point gap — .018 to .022.
Spark plug gap — .035.
Free movement or end play in clutch pedal — 1" minimum.

MODEL A FORD ENGINE BOLT SIZES & QUANTITIES

Main Bearings —
  4—½ x 5½ bolts; front & center.
  2—½ x 4 bolts; rear.
Timing Gear Housing —
  6—⅜ x 1⅛ cap screws w/ lockwashers; gear case.
  1—⅜ x 1⅛ cap screw w/ special head for timing ignition (Head 5/16 x ⅝).
Flywheel — 4—7/16 x ¾ SAE cap screws w/ drilled head.
Clutch Housing Plate —
  2—¼ x ½ cap screws w/ lockwashers.
Oil Pan — 20—5/16 x ¾ cap screws w/ lockwashers.
Valve Cover Plate —
  10—5/16 x ¾ cap screws and lockwashers.
Cylinder Head — 12—7/16 SAE nuts.
Oil Return Pipe —
  2—5/16 x 1¼ cap screws w/ copper washers.
Manifold, In. & Exh. —
  4—7/16 SAE nuts w/ thick flat washers.
Starting Motor —
  3—⅜ x 1 cap screws w/ lockwashers; 3 steel shim spacer washers between flange and pad.
Transmission Assembly —
  11—⅜ x 1 cap screws w/ lockwashers.
Steering Column —
  2—½ x 1 SAE cap screws w/ lockwashers; column to chassis.
  2—½ x 1 Fillister head machine screws; cowl support clamp.

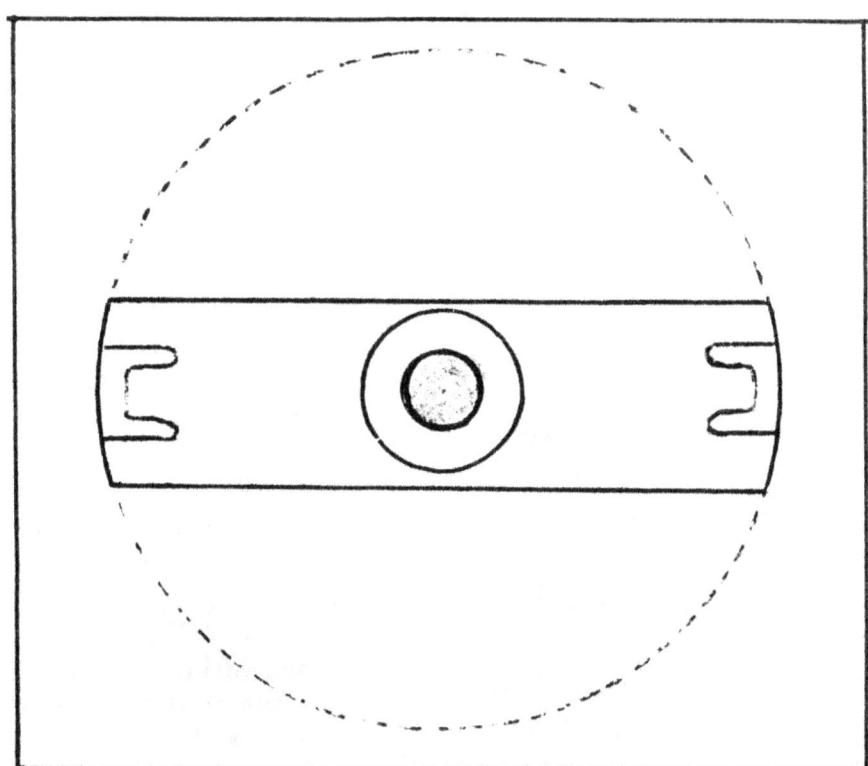

FIGURE 95. A TEST CAP FOR CHECKING DISTRIBUTOR POINTS IN ACTION.

To observe action of the breaker points of a MODEL A distributor while the engine is running, temporarily install a cap having the sides cut away as shown. This can easily be made from a spare cap using an ordinary hack saw.

INSTRUCTION SHEET
For Servicing
ZENITH CARBURETOR (FORD MODELS A & B)

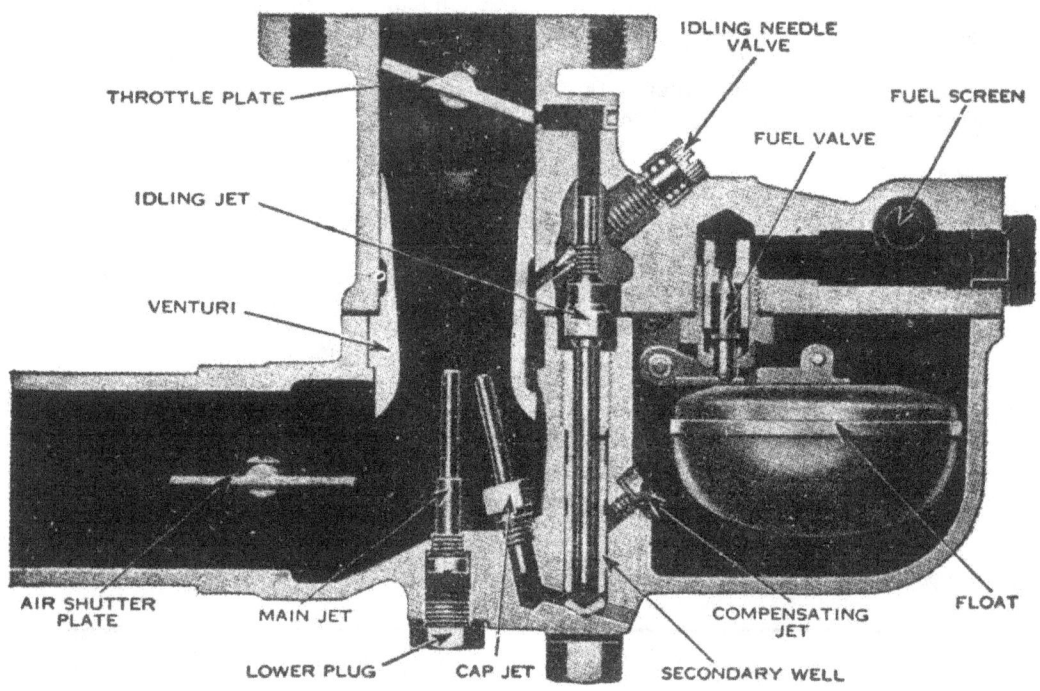

1. Unscrew bolt that holds throttle barrel to body and take the two halves of carburetor apart.

2. From lower part of body remove lower plug, then main jet. Also compensator and cap jet. On model "B" also remove power jet.

3. Remove Secondary well and clean side holes.

4. From upper or throttle barrel remove float and needle and seat, fuel screen, idle jet, idle adjusting needle.

5. Clean all parts in a good cleaning compound and blow out with compressed air. Scrape carbon away from idle port in inside of throttle barrel by throttle valve.

6. Re-assemble using all parts in kits. Be sure to use all new gaskets.

7. Set fuel level on model "A" 5/8 of an inch and on Model "B" 33/64 of an inch below machined surface of lower body. If no fuel level gauge is available hold the throttle barrel in an inverted position and regulate float until surface of float nearest the machined surface is parallel.

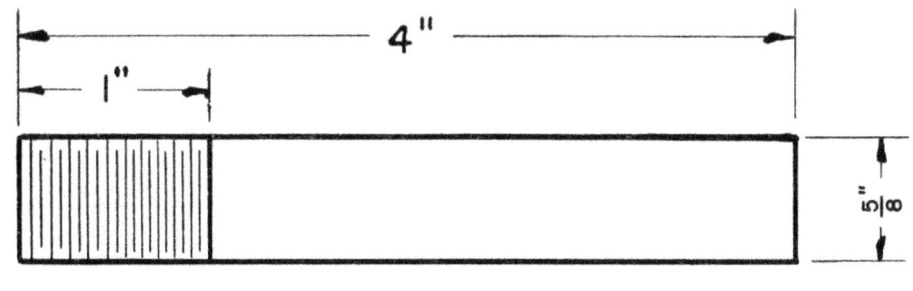

THREAD TO FIT STUD IN BODY, SIZE $\frac{5}{8}"$ x 18

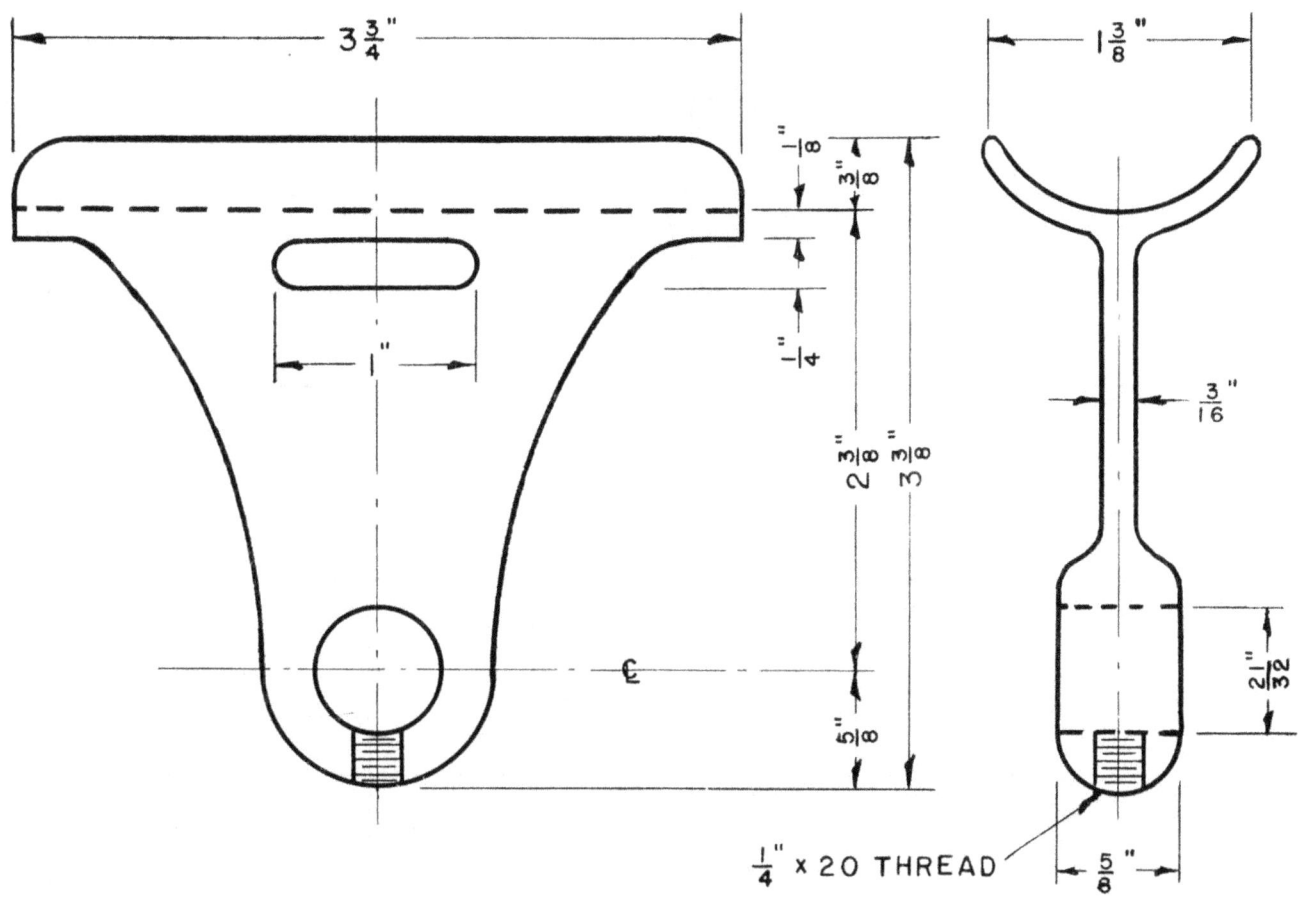

SCALE: 1" = 1"

NOTE:- WHILE THESE WERE ORIGINALLY CAST IN BRASS, DUPLICATES CAN BE MADE BY BRAZING OR WELDING TOGETHER THREE FABRICATED PIECES.

BOW BRACKET

FOR SUPPORTING TOP BOWS WHEN FOLDED DOWN ON THE MODEL A FORD PHAETON

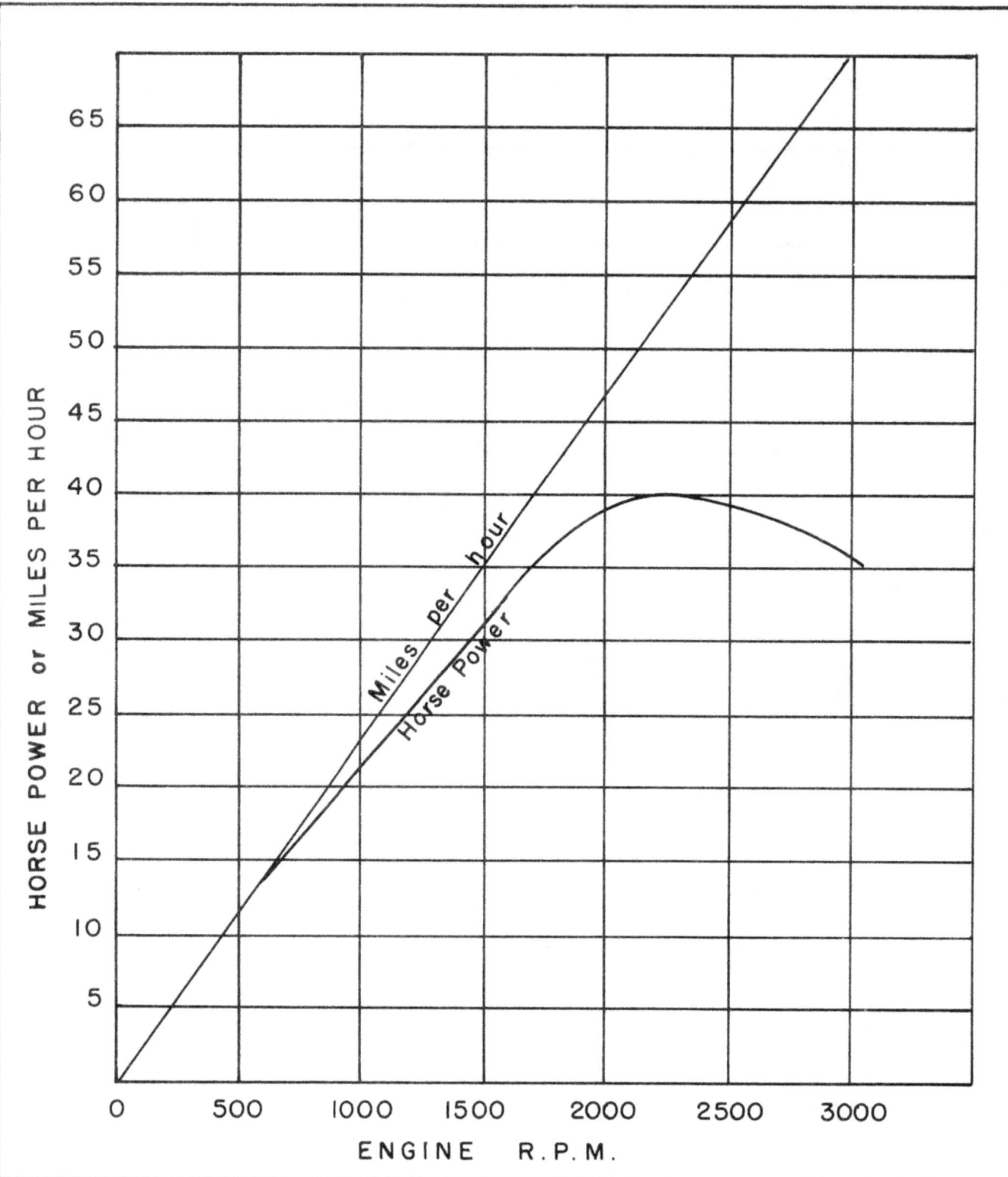

FORD MODEL A COLOR EQUIVALENTS

Color equivalents are based on DuPont finishes available at DuPont refinish distributors throughout the United States. Dulux finishes are air dry enamels while Duco finishes are lacquers. The **original Model A's were finished in pyroxylin lacquers** except for the fenders which were finished in black dipping enamel.
*Available in metallic quality only.

MUNSELL CODE	COLOR	"DUCO"	"DULUX"
5 YR 5/11	Yukon Yellow		93-003
5 YR 6/13	Pegex Orange		93-1021
5 Y 8/5	Medium Cream	725	246-81373
5 Y 7/6	Cream	1559	246-57336
10 BGB 1/3	Blue Rock Green	2204-H*	2204-H*
5 G 2/2	Rock Moss Green	923-G	246-81572-G
5 G 3/4	Balsam Green		93-1855
5 BG 2/4	Vagabond Green		93-81872
5 Y 5/2	Arabian Sand Light		246-31470
10 YGY 3/2	Commercial Drab		93-35648
10 YRY 5/3	Pembroke Gray		None
10 GBG 4/2	Dawn Gray Light		None
5 G 3/1	Bonnie Gray	1293	246-57107
5 R 1/10	Rubelite Red	1497-M	1497-M
5 R 3/14	Vermilion		93-24119
5 PB 00/2	Lombard Blue		246-55106
10 BGB 1/2	Niagara Blue Dark		246-35961
10 BGB 2/4	Niagara Blue Light	783	246-55446
5 BG 2/2	Gun Metal Blue		93-81872
10 BGB 3/4	Duchess Blue	1345-G	246-57118-G
10 YRY 2/2	Mountain Brown		93-3836
10 GBG 2/4	Valley Green		246-34918
10 GYG 2/2	Highland Green		246-34116
10 GYG 3/1	Kewanee Green	785	246-71075
10 GYG 2/1	Elkspointe Green		246-35859
10 GBG 2/3	L'Anse Green Dark		93-6621
5 G 4/3	Lawn Green	662-G	246-62201-G
5 YR 3/5	Phoenix Brown		93-81412
10 YRY 5/4	Manila Brown	837*	202-55505*
5 YR 0/1	Thorne Brown		246-30340
10 YRY 3/1	Copra Drab	884	246-55551
5 Y 3/2	Chickle Drab		None
5 Y 4/2	Arabian Sand Dark		None
10 BGB 2/3	Washington Blue		246-34760
Neutral 1	Stone Gray Deep		246-51252
5 BG 3/2	Dawn Gray Dark	602	246-55134
10 YRY 4/3	Stone Brown		246-35922
5 GY 1/2	Brewster Green		246-54723
10 YRY 0/2	Seal Brown	658	246-60371
5 Y 7/7	Bronson Yellow		None
5 Y 2/1	Moleskin Brown Light		93-6846
5 R 0/3	Ford Maroon		None
10 BPB 00/2	Lombard Blue	914	246-81580
5 GY 3/3	Kewanee Green		93-546
5 YR 4/3	No. 1 Cord and No. 3 Striped Cloth—Light		246-81467
5 YR 3/1	No. 2 Mohair and No. 3 Striped Cloth—Dark		246-50964
5 YR 3/2	No. 4 Mohair		246-81467
10 YRY 4/3	No. 5 Leather, two toned textured: light area		None
10 YRY 0/1	No. 5 Leather, two toned textured: dark area		None
10 YRY 1/3	No. 6 Leather		93-3836

MODEL "A" FORD PAINT LIST as prepared by Ditzler Paint Company:

ALL 1929 MODELS

	Upper	Lower
Tudor and Coupe	Chelsea Blue (IM-120)	Bonnie Gray (IM-116)
	Rock Moss Green (IM-117)	Vagabond Green (IM-122)
	Seal Brown (IM-118)	Rose Beige (IM-119)
	Black	Andalusite Blue (IM-121)
Fordor	Chelsea Blue (IM-120)	Bonnie Gray (IM-116)
	Rock Moss Green (IM-117)	Vagabond Green (IM-122)
	Seal Brown (IM-118)	Rose Beige (IM-119)
	Andalusite Blue (IM-121)	Aandalusite Blue
Cabriolet	Seal Brown (IM-118)	Cigarette Cream (IM-451)
Phaeton and Roadster	Bonnie Gray (IM-116)	Bonnie Gray
	Rose Beige (IM-119)	Rose Beige
	Andalusite Blue (IM-121)	Andalusite Blue
	Balsam Green (IM-124)	Balsam Green
Taxicab	Medium Cream (IM-125)	Duchess Blue (IM-123)
	Medium Cream (IM-125)	Balsam Green (IM-124)
Town Car	Black	Brewster Green (IM-1017)
	Black	Mulberry Maroon (IM-1046)
	Black	Thorne Brown (IM-283)
Town Sedan	Rock Moss Green (IM-117)	Vagabond Green (IM-122)
	Rock Moss Green (IM-117)	Lawn Green (IM-159)
Commercial Jobs	Rock Moss Green (IM-117)	Rock Moss Green (IM-117)

1930 MODELS

	Upper	Lower
Tudor Sedan	Chicle Drab (IM-91)	Copra Drab (IM-440)
	Kewanee Green (IM-546)	Elk Point Green (IM-543)
	Black	Andalusite Blue (IM-121)
	Thorne Brown (IM-283)	Thorne Brown
Two and Three Window Fordor Sedan	Thorne Brown (IM-283)	Thorne Brown
	Chicle Drab (IM-91)	Copra Drab (IM-446)
Sedan	Kewanee Green (IM-546)	Elk Point Green (IM-543)
	Black	Ford Maroon (IM-1011)
	Andalusite Blue (IM-121)	Andalusite Blue
Town Sedan	Black	Ford Maroon (IM-1011)
	Chicle Drab (IM-91)	Copra Drab (IM-440)
Phaeton and Roadster	Thorne Brown (IM-283)	Thorne Brown
	Kewanee Green (IM-546)	Elk Point Green (IM-543)
	Chicle Drab (IM-91)	Copra Drab (IM-440)
	Andalusite Blue (IM-121)	Andalusite Blue
Sport Coupe	Kewanee Green (IM-546)	Elk Point Green (IM-543)
	Black	Andalusite Blue (IM-121)
	Chicle Drab (IM-91)	Copra Drab (IM-440)
	Thorne Brown (IM-283)	Thorne Brown
Standard Coupe	Andalusite Blue (IM-121)	Andalusite Blue
	Kewanee Green (IM-546)	Elk Point Green (IM-543)
	Chicle Drab (IM-91)	Copra Drab (IM-440)
	Thorne Brown	Thorne Brown
	Andalusite Blue (IM-121)	Andalusite Blue
	Seal Brown (IM-118)	Bronson Yellow
Convertible Cabriolet	Moleskin Brown Lt. (IM-544)	Elk Point Green (IM-543)
	Kewanee Green (IM-546)	

1931 MODELS

	Upper	Lower
Tudor and Standard Fordor	Black	Lonbard Blue (IM-1009)
Standard Coupe and Sport Coupe	Thorne Brown (IM-283)	Thorne Brown
	Elk Point Green (IM-543)	Chicle Drab (IM-91)
	Cobra Drab (IM-440)	Chicle Drab
DeLuxe Cabriolet	Elk Point Green (IM-543)	Kewanee Green (IM-546)
2-Window Fordor DeLuxe	Copra Drab (IM-440)	Chicle Drab (IM-91)
Coupe, DeLuxe Sedan, Town	Black	Brewster Green Medium (IM-1017)
Sedan, Victoria Coupe	Black	Ford Maroon (IM-1011)
DeLuxe Phaeton	Black	Brewster Green Medium (IM-1017)
DeLuxe Roadster	Moulding—Stone Deep Gray (IM-1015)	Stone Brown (IM-1016)
	Moulding—Riviera Blue (IM-1013)	Washington Blue Medium (IM-1014)
Phaeton and Roadster	Black	Lombard Blue (IM-1009)
	Black	Thorne Brown (IM-283)
	Moulding—Elk Point Green (IM-543)	Kewanee Green (IM-546)
	Moulding—Copra Drab (IM-440)	Chicle Drab (IM-91)
Cabriolet	Seal Brown (IM-118)	Bronson Yellow (IM-545)
	Lombard Blue (IM-1009)	Lombard Blue
	Moleskin Brown (IM-544)	Moleskin Brown
Commercial Jobs	Blue Rock Green (IM-1012)	Blue Rock Green

The above (IM Numbers) can be converted by any Ditzler paint dealer into a formula that the desired colors may be made from.

Sherwin-Williams Color Formulae for the following automobile lacquers (stated by volume):

Riviera Blue
41 Parts Bone Black (Opex No. 31111)
33 Parts Prussian Blue (Opex No. 31044)
24 Parts Auto White (Opex No. 31001)
2 Parts Toning Yellow (Opex No. 31163)

* * * *

Washington Blue
61 Parts Prussian Blue (Opex No. 31044)
30 Parts Bone Black (Opex No. 31111)
9 Parts Auto White (Opex No. 31001)
Touch   Toning Yellow (Opex No. 31163)

* * * *

Tacoma Cream
88 Parts Auto White (Opex No. 31001)
12 Parts Toning Yellow (Opex No. 31163)
Touch   Red Oxide
Touch   Ultramarine Blue

Tacoma Cream was used on the wheels, and a double pin stripe in Tacoma Cream ran over the Riviera Blue moulding reveals.

Although these mixes are for lacquer, they can be used for enamel by substituting comparable shades of mixing colors in enamel material.

The 1931 Model A Ford DeLuxe Roadster in the original factory combinations of Riviera Blue, Washington Blue, Tacoma Cream, and Black, was painted as follows:

Washington Blue was used on the hood and body, doors, rumble seat deck lid, etc.

Riviera Blue was used on the moulding reveals along the side of the hood, along tops of doors, and around the body. Two moulding reveals sweep down the rear of the body and along side the rumble seat deck lid.

Black was used on the fenders and splash aprons, bumper brackets, trunk carrier, etc.

CHAPTER XII
LOCATING MODEL A ENGINE TROUBLE

Location of the Ford Model A Power Plant Troubles Made Easy

An Authoritative Chart Outlining the Common Derangements
That Interfere With Proper Action of Engine and Auxiliary Systems

Chart Arranged by VICTOR W. PAGÉ, M. E., Author of "The Ford Models T and A Cars" Etc., Etc.

MOTOR WILL NOT SPEED UP
Air Choke Valve in Carburetor Air Pipe Stuck Closed.
Pistons Binding in Cylinder.
Not Enough Oil in Engine Base.
Bent or Sticking Valve Stem.
Too Much Play in Valve Operating Plungers.
Too Much Space Between Valve Stems and Push Rods.
Valves Timed Late.
Spark Timed Late.
Throttle Stuck Closed.
Timer Stuck in Retard Position.
Binding Contact Bell Crank.
Dragging Brakes in Hubs.
Driving System Parts Not in Alignment.

MOTOR WILL NOT STOP
Throttle Remains Open.
Spark Interrupting Switch Out of Order.
Incandescent Carbon Deposits Fire Charge.
Overheated Engine.

MOTOR SPEEDS UP SUDDENLY
Timer Casing Advanced.
Clutch Slipping or Released.
Throttle Has Jarred Open.

MOTOR RUNS IRREGULARLY OR MISFIRES
a—Defects in Motor Mechanism.
    Carbon Deposits in Combustion Chamber.
    Weak, or Broken Valve Springs.
    Sticky Valve Stems.
    Carbon Under Valve Heads.
    Worn Push Rod or Guide.
    No Clearance Between Valve Stem and Plungers.
    Air Leak in Inlet Piping.
    Broken Cylinder Head Gasket.
    Air Leak Through Inlet Valve Guides.

b—Faults in Fuel Supply System.
    Carburetor Float Chamber Getting Dry.
    Water or Dirt in Gasoline.
    Poor Gasoline Adjustment.
    Not Enough Gasoline in Float Chamber.
    Too Much Gasoline, Carburetor Flooding.
    Poor Gasoline.

c—Ignition System Faults.
    Loose Wiring or Terminals Anywhere.
    Broken Spark Plug Insulator.
    Spark Plug Points Sooted or Oily.
    Wrong Spark Gap at Plug Points.
    Leaking Secondary Distributor Head.
    Prematurely Grounded Primary Wire.
    Battery Running Down.
    Poor Adjustment of Contact Points at Timer.
    Wire Broken Inside of Insulation.
    Pitted Platinum Points on Timer.
    Weak Spring, Timer Bell Crank.
    Dirt in Battery Timer.
    Worn Points in Timer.
    Gummed Oil in Timer or Distributor.
    Defective Condenser in Coil.

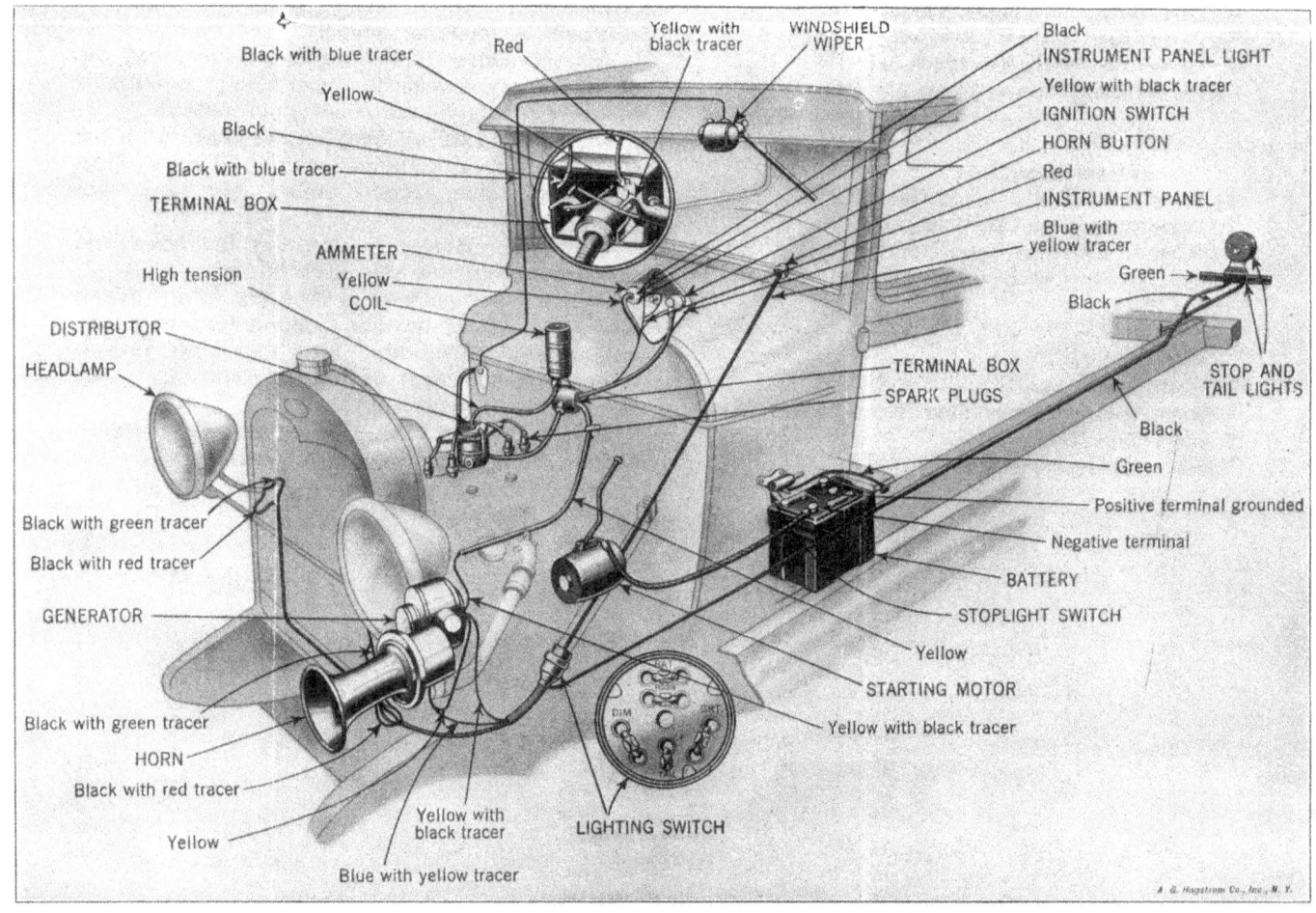

Showing Disposition of Starting Motor, Battery and Generator on Ford Model A Car

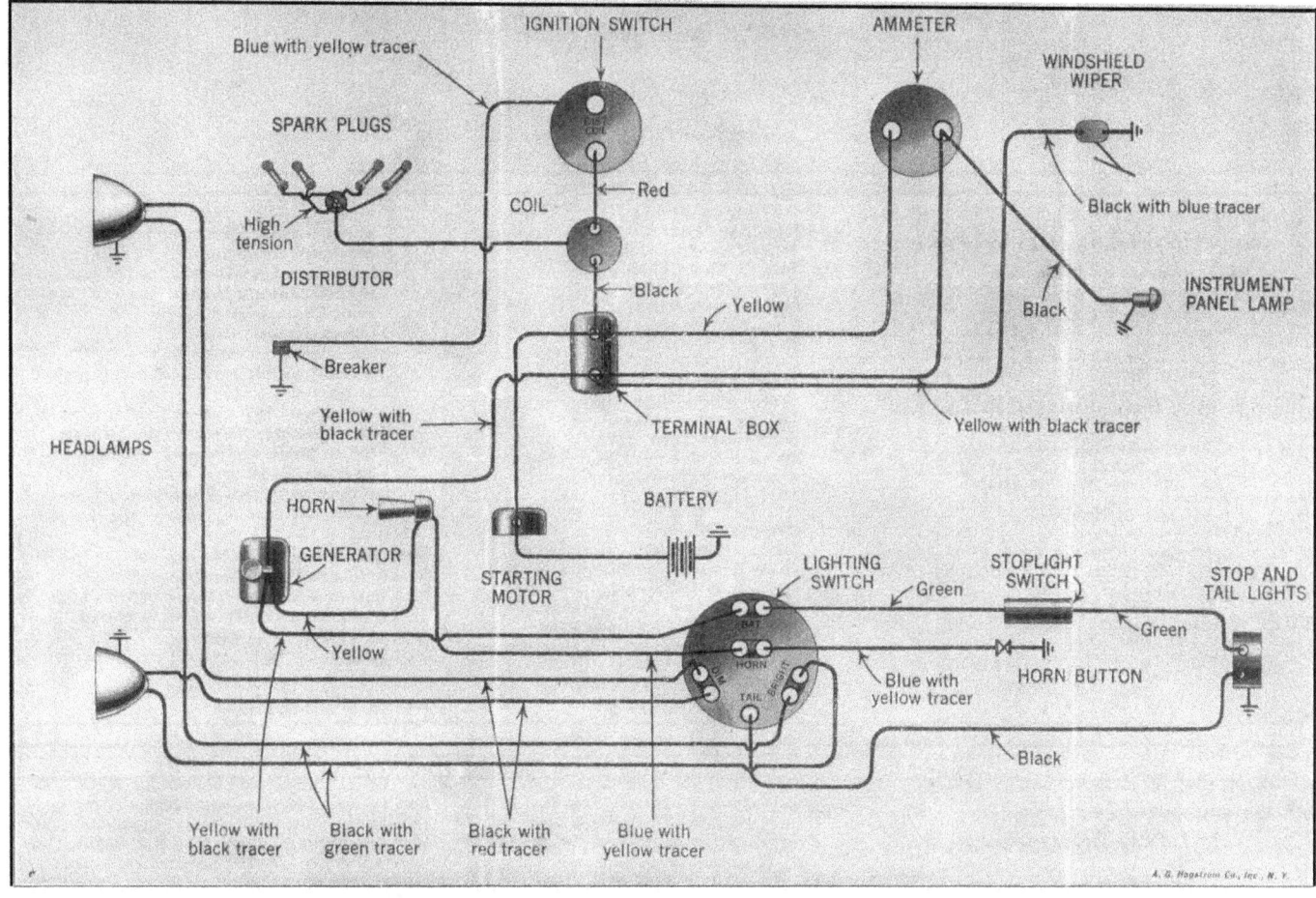

Wiring Diagram of Ford Model A Lighting, Ignition and Starting System Showing All Units

MOTOR STOPS WITHOUT WARNING

Broken Primary Wire.
Broken Timer Spring (Rare).
Gasoline Shutoff Valve Jarred Closed.
Gasoline Supply Pipe Clogged.
No Gasoline in Tank.
Spray Nozzle Stopped Up.
Water in Spray Nozzle.
Particles of Carbon or Oil Between Spark Plug Points.
Ignition Short Circuited by Ground in Wire.
Air Lock in Gasoline Pipe or Tank.
Battery Wire Loose at Either Terminal.
Inlet Valve Stuck Open.
Pistons Seized on Account of Defective Oiling.
Bent or Broken Camshaft or Crankshaft (Rare).
Seized Main Bearings (Rare).
Insufficient Lubrication.
Flywheel Wedged by Foreign Matter in Engine Base (Rare).
Sheared Key in Crankshaft Gear Operating Valve Mechanism (Rare).

MOTOR STOPS GRADUALLY

Fuel Supply Pipe Partially Clogged.
Air Vent in Tank Filler Cap Stopped Up.
Float Needle Valve Stuck.
Water or Dirt in Spray Nozzle.
Mixture Adjusting Needle Jarred Loose.
Loose Terminal at Battery.
Valves Stuck Open.
Motor Overheating Due to Defective Oiling or Cooling.
Spark Advance Rod Broken.
Throttle Rod Breaks.
Sticking Contact Points.

MOTOR RACES

Control Rods Broken.
Defective Induction Pipe Joints.
Leaky Carburetor Flange Packing.
Throttle Not Closing.
Timer Stuck in Advance Position.
Clutch Slips (in High Speed).

MOTOR NOISY IN ACTION

a—Mechanical Depreciation Producing Knocking.
  Foreign Matter in Engine, Such as Loose Nut in Engine Base.
  Carbon Deposits in Combustion Chamber.
  Incandescent Spark Plug Points or Carbon Particles.
  High Piston.
  Loose Wrist Pin Bearings.
  Loose Connecting Rod Big End Bearings.
  Worn Main Bearings.
  Piston Worn, Permitting Side Slap.
  Cylinder Worn Out of Round.
  Cylinder Head Retention Bolts Loose.
  Play in Valve Operating Mechanism.
  Timing Gears Worn.
  Loose Flywheel.
  Poor Oil or Lack of Oil.
  Piston Rings Tight.
  Broken Ball in Gear Set.

b—Mixture Troubles.
  Too Much Gasoline, Mixture Rich.
  Carburetor Float Chamber Flooding.

c—Ignition Troubles.
  Spark Timed Too Early.

d—Other Causes of Knocking.
  Climbing Steep Hills on High Gear.
  Overheating Due to Defective Cooling.

e—Hissing and Squeaking Sounds.
  Broken Insulation on Spark Plug.
  Spark Plug Leaks.
  Loose Joint Between Motor and Exhaust Manifold.
  Valve Spring Chamber Covers Loose.
  Leaking Cylinder Head Packing.
  Poor Lubrication (Causes Squeaking).
  Muffler Leaking or Ruptured.
  Broken Piston Rings (Blowing Sound).
  Tight Piston Rings (Scraping Sound).

f—Popping or Blowing Back in Carburetor.
  Incorrectly Timed Inlet Valves.
  Inlet Valve Not Seating.
  Defective Inlet Valve Spring.
  Dirt Under Inlet Valve Seat.
  Not Enough Gasoline (Open Needle Valve).
  Spark Retards Too Much.
  Contact Points on Timer Pitted.
  Weak Battery

g—Muffler Explosions.
  Mixture Not Exploding Regularly.
  Exhaust Valve Sticking.
  Dirt Under Exhaust Valve Seat.
  Sticking Breaker Points.
  Ruptured Muffler.

h—Grinding Noises.
  Worn Timing Gears.
  Defective Cylinder Lubrication.
  Worn Driving Gears.
  Worn Change Speed Gearing (Not Noticed on Direct Drive).

COPYRIGHT 1928 BY THE NORMAN W. HENLEY PUBLISHING CO., NEW YORK, N.Y.

MOTOR WILL NOT START OR STARTS HARD

a—Defects in Motor Mechanism.
    Leaky Head Gasket.
    Water or Rust in Cylinders.
    Seized Pistons or Dry Pistons.
    Piston Rings Gummed to Cylinder.
    Valve Stuck (Rare).
    Pump Impeller Frozen (Winter Only).
    Valve Gears Out in Time.
    Broken Crankshaft (Rare).
    Broken Exhaust Valve Spring.
    Broken Inlet Valve Spring.
    Broken Timing Gears (Rare).

b—Fuel System Faults.
    No Gasoline in Tank.
    No Gasoline in Carburetor Float Chamber.
    Old or Stale Gasoline.
    Tank Shut-Off Closed.
    Clogged Filter Screen.
    Fuel Supply Pipe Clogged by Dirt.
    Pipe Clogged by Water.
    Gasoline Level Too Low.
    Gasoline Level Too High (Flooding).
    Filler Cap Vent Clogged.
    Broken Choke Control.
    Bent or Stuck Float Lever.
    Choke Control Stuck.
    Loose or Defective Inlet Manifold.
    Not Enough Gasoline at Jet.
    Cylinders Flooded with Gas.
    Leaky Float (Causes Flooding).
    Water in Carburetor Spray Nozzle.
    Dirt in Float Chamber.
    Gas Mixture Too Lean.
    Carburetor Frozen (Winter Only).
    Sediment Bulb Full of Dirt.
    Float Valve Stuck.

c—Ignition System Troubles.
    Ignition Switch-Off.
    Loose Terminal on Coil or Switch.
    Ignition Wire Shorted.
    Plug Defective (No Spark at Plugs).
    Broken Spark Plug Insulation.
    Carbon Deposits or Oil Between Plug Points.
    Spark Plugs Points Too Near Together or Too Far Apart.
    Short Circuited Secondary Coil.
    Stuck Breaker Points.
    Short Circuit in Distributor.
    Storage Battery Weak.
    Poor Contacts at Timer.
    Timer Points Dirty.
    Poor Contact at Switch.
    Primary Wires Broken or Short Circuited
    Battery Grounded by Short Circuited Wire.
    Storage Battery Connections Broken.
    Loose Battery Wire or Terminal.
    Defects in Induction Coil.
    Corroded Battery Terminals.
    Ignition Timing Wrong, Spark Too Late or Too Early.
    Defective Platinum Points in Timer.
    Broken Timer Contact Spring.
    No Contact at Points.
    Platinum Contact Points Burnt or Pitted.
    Contact Maker Lever Stuck.
    Dirt or Water in Timer Casing.
    Poor Battery Ground Wire.
    Defective Ignition Lock.

MOTOR LOSES POWER

a—Causes of Poor Compression.
    Loose Spark Plugs.
    Defective Cylinder Head Gasket.
    Cracked Piston or Cylinder (Rare).
    Leaky Valves (Regrind).
    Warped Valve Heads.
    Piston Ring Joints in Line.
    Head Casting Loose on Cylinder.
    Worn Piston Rings.

b—Other Causes of Lost Power.
    Exhaust Valve Lift Insufficient.
    Inlet Valve Lift Insufficient.
    Choked Muffler.
    Carbon Deposits.
    Tight Bearings.
    Cylinder Dry or Overheated.
    Oil Too Light.
    Oil Carbonizes at Too Low Temperature.
    Overheating Due to Driving with Retarded Spark.
    Overheating Due to Racing Motor on Low Speed Gear.
    Overheating Due to Too Rich Mixture.
    Oil Feed Interrupted.
    Fan Belt Loose or Broken.
    No Water in Radiator.
    Pump Defective.

Note.—All causes contributing to irregular motor action also produce lost power.

STARTING AND LIGHTING SYSTEM TROUBLES

IF STARTER WILL NOT TURN

1. See that starter pedal is not sticking and goes all the way down. Disconnect storage battery under seat, if pedal sticks.
2. Note whether starter gear goes into engagement. If starter spins, "nurse" the pedal until gear engages. In all automatic shift systems make sure spring is not broken or pinion is not stuck to thread on shaft.
3. See that main leads between battery switch and starter are firmly connected, especially at the battery and starting switch.
4. Battery may be discharged.
5. Start with crank and report promptly to Service Station.

IF STARTER TURNS MOTOR, BUT MOTOR WILL NOT FIRE

1. Do not continue to "churn" motor, but check over motor conditions. See that—
    Ignition switch is in proper position.
    Throttle lever is open about one and one-half inches.
    Air choke lever is closed (in cool or cold weather).
    There is gasoline in the carburetor.
    Gasoline line cock is open.

See if any of the Ignition System troubles under heading "Motor Will Not Start" exist.

2. With a very cold motor it may take some time to get an ignitable mixture into the cylinders, but if the air choke valve almost entirely closes the carburetor intake a strong suction will draw gasoline into cylinders as effectively as priming.

3. In moderate weather continued churning with the air choke closed will cause cylinders to flood. To clear motor open wide the air choke and throttle levers.

ALL LIGHTS GO OUT—IGNITION FAILS—STARTING MOTOR DEAD—The cause for this is: (1) A loose connection either at battery terminals, at "battery" side of starting switch, or at point where battery is grounded to the frame of the car. (2) A loose connection at motor side of starting switch or at starting motor and the wire between the switches broken. (3) Loose connection at motor side of starting switch or at starting motor and a fuse burnt out.

ALL LIGHTS GO OUT—IGNITION FAILS—STARTING MOTOR O. K.—A short or open circuit in the wire between the starting switch and fuse block or the fuse being burnt out. Look first to see if this fuse is intact. If the fuse is burnt out make a careful examination—for grounds—of the wiring between the switch, the lamps and the ignition distributor before replacing with new fuse. See that all connections on the terminal block are tight.

ALL LIGHTS GO OUT—IGNITION AND STARTING MOTOR O. K.—It is evident that this trouble is confined to open circuits between the lighting switch and the lamps, loose connections at lighting switch or at lamp, or burned-out bulbs.

IGNITION FAILS—LIGHTS AND STARTING MOTOR O. K.—This trouble may be traced to loose connections at the ignition switch, coil or ignition distributor, poor grounding of the switch (one wire system) or open circuits or short circuits between the ignition switch and timer.

GENERATOR TEST—A simple test to determine if the ignition generator is properly operating, if the ammeter pointer shows no indication, is first, switch all lights on with engine idle; second, start engine and run same reasonably fast. If lights brighten after starting engine it proves that the ignition generator is properly delivering current. This test must necessarily be conducted in the dark, either in garage or outside, preferably at night time. Ammeter should indicate charge if in working order.

ONE LIGHT GOES DIM—The more probable causes of this are a defective bulb or connection at the lamp. If these are O. K. make an examination for short circuits in the wiring to the lamp.

ONE LIGHT FLICKERS—Loose or frayed connection at lamp or at switch. An intermittent ground or short circuit in the wiring to the lamp. Bulb loose in socket.

TAIL LIGHT GOES OUT—Look first for a burned-out bulb. Then see that the wire to the lamp is not broken, that connections at switch and lamp are tight and that the body of the lamp is making good electrical connection with the frame of the car, if a one wire circuit is employed.

COWL LIGHT GOES OUT—Make an examination, same as in preceding paragraph, of cowl light circuit. If stop light does not work, be sure to inspect switch, which is separate from that controling other lamps.

HEAD LIGHTS GO OUT—Make examination of head light circuit.

ONE HEAD LIGHT GOES OUT—It is evident that this trouble is confined to an open circuit between the junction and the lamp, bad connection at lamp, burned-out bulb, or frame of lamp not grounded properly (one wire system).

FUSES BLOW OUT—This indicates a short circuit in lighting circuit. Test all in order starting with stop light and switch.

Chart Arranged by VICTOR W. PAGÉ, M. E., Author of "The Ford Models T and A Cars" Etc., Etc.

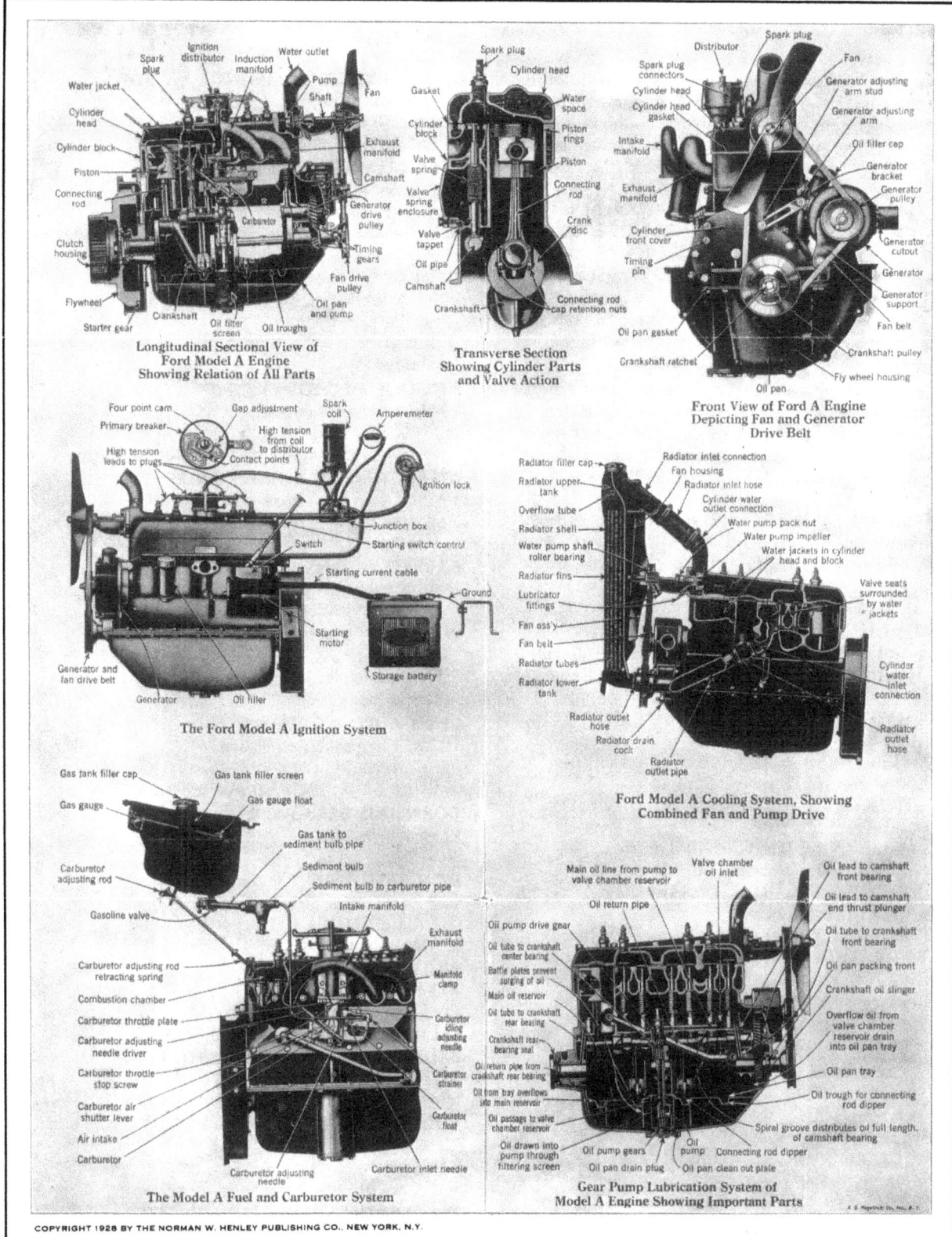

COPYRIGHT 1928 BY THE NORMAN W. HENLEY PUBLISHING CO., NEW YORK, N.Y.

INSTRUCTIONS FOR USE

Ford engine troubles can be easily identified by readily recognized symptoms, and the same symptoms are often produced by widely differing causes. The defective conditions more apt to obtain are enumerated in tabular form. In most cases the method of repairing the defect is apparent. Those not understanding the mechanism sufficiently to be able to use this condensed statement of common troubles or those who do not know how to repair the defects enumerated will find the elementary text-book, "The Ford Models T and A Cars, Construction, Operation and Repair,"* which the chart supplements (printed by the same publisher), of value in getting complete knowledge of Ford car construction, maintenance, and repairing. The novice should attempt to locate troubles systematically, and the logical enumeration of defective conditions should help him as well as the more expert. *[Price $2.00]

For example, if the motor runs irregularly this condition is apparent at once. The points needing inspection are enumerated under that head, and if followed systematically the trouble can be found by elimination, even by the inexpert. The common troubles are all classed under easily recognized main symptoms, such as Lost Power, Noisy Operation, Starting and Lighting System Faults, etc.

THIS CHART IS COPYRIGHTED AND PUBLISHED BY THE NORMAN W. HENLEY PUBLISHING CO., 2 W. 45th ST., NEW YORK. PRICE 35 CENTS. SUPPLIED IN QUANTITIES AT SPECIAL PRICES

CHAPTER XIII
PARTS SUPPLIERS AND SOURCES

While the Ford Motor Company and the Ford dealers have *not* maintained stocks of MODEL A parts for many years, it is possible that your local Ford dealer *may* have a few parts still remaining on his shelves, and nearly every Ford dealer can arrange to supply a rebuilt MODEL A engine on order.

Many individuals have acquired parts which they offer for sale by mail order as a part of their antique automobile hobby activity. Some few of these have built this activity up to the proportions of small business enterprises and publish periodic lists of available parts. Others simply specialize in certain parts or accessories, some of which are being newly manufactured to meet the increasing demands of MODEL A enthusiasts.

MODEL A parts may also be located through the classified advertisement sections of the publications of many Ford and antique automobile clubs in America.

Several of the major mail order houses still list MODEL A (and Model T) Ford parts in their catalogs.

Here, without recommendation of any kind, are alphabetical listings of the several major club publications, the many individuals, and the three major mail order houses offering MODEL A Ford parts and accessories:

1. CLUB PUBLICATIONS

These are not the only clubs devoted to the automotive hobby, but these are large clubs publishing regular magazines, and offering many membership benefits:

The ANTIQUE AUTOMOBILE
    published bi-monthly by:
    The Antique Automobile Club of America, Inc.*
    Hershey Museum, Hershey, Penna.

The BULB HORN
    published quarterly by:
    The Veteran Motor Car Club of America
    15 Newton Street, Brookline 46, Mass.

The HORSELESS CARRIAGE GAZETTE
    published bi-monthly by:
    The Horseless Carriage Club of America, Inc.
    7730 South Western Ave., Los Angeles 47, Calif.

The MARC NEWS
    published monthly by:
    The Model "A" Restorer's Club
    P. O. Box 615, Zanesville, Ohio

The RESTORER
    published quarterly by:
    The Model A Ford Club of America, Inc.
    6924 San Fernando Road, Glendale, Calif.

*This club caters to all types of antique, classic, and production cars and has a division for Model A Fords.

2. INDIVIDUAL SUPPLIERS

When writing to a supplier be sure to list specifically the parts you want and identify them by Ford number, if possible. Remember that this is usually a hobby on the parts of suppliers, so be sure to enclose a stamped, self-addressed envelope for a reply. Remember, too, that existing supplies of these parts are limited; do not be surprised if some of the parts you want are gone by the time you write!

AETNA RUBBER COMPANY
108 Broad Street
Boston 10, Mass.
    Tops & curtains ready-made

O. R. ALLMAN
285 DeSmet Drive
Florisant, Missouri
    Parts list available. Has new back & seat cushions for A & T Fords.

GEORGE DE ANGELIS
9830 Allen Road
Allen Park, Michigan
    Duplicate FORD patent date plates & ignition switch plates only.

ANTIQUE ACCESSORY SHOP
2125 Lacrosse Avenue
St. Paul 6, Minn.
    Flying Quail mascot for radiator cap only.

ATLANTIC AUTO & TRUCK SALES
19020 South Figueroa
Gardena, Calif.
    Used parts for all makes of cars.

BARRETT & SONS, INC.
Main Street
Matawan, New Jersey

WILLIAM F. BEAVER
2724 Pasteur Avenue
Overland 14, Missouri
    Large Stock. Parts list available.

BEN'S AUTO WRECKING
10225 Glenoaks Boulevard
Pacoima, Calif.
    Large Stock. Parts list available.

CORNELIUS BERBOWER
Rt. #3
Newton, Illinois

DON BESTLAND
122 East Laurel Street
Glendale 5, Calif.
    Many new parts.

BILL BITTMANN
4154 North Drake
Chicago, Illinois
    Large Stock. Parts list available.

BRUER AUTO PARTS & REBUILDERS
1900 Blaine Street
Springfield, Missouri

ROBERT C. BURCHILL
2316 17th Avenue
Port Huron, Mich.
    Parts Catalog, 50c.

WALT CANN
324 North Fullerton Avenue
Montclair, New Jersey.

COMPETITION ACCESSORIES
704 Washington Ave., Box 141
Iowa Falls, Iowa.
    New Moto-Meters; Clock mirrors.

ROBERT J. CARINI
67 Denslow Road
Glastonbury, Conn.
    Send your want list.

G. C. CHEATHAM
708 Robinson Drive
Birmingham 6, Alabama.

KENNETH COULTER
Sevierville Road
Marysville, Tenn.
  Send your want list.

JOE CUZELIS
20724 Fairview Drive
Dearborn, Mich.

DRAWBRIDGE AUTO SUPPLY
Broadkiln River, Rt. 14
Milton, Delaware.
  Send your want list.

EDWARD DUDIK
5810 - 44th Avenue
Hyattsville, Maryland
  Send your want list.

EGGE MACHINE COMPANY
(Nels Egge)
7704 South Main Street
Los Angeles 3, Calif.
  Manufacturer of aluminum pistons.

ELMER'S AUTO PARTS
Webster, New York.
  Send your want list.

BILLY VON ESSER
3307 West Irving Park
Chicago 18, Illinois.

BOB FIGGE
1916 North Wilson
Hollywood, Calif.

DENNY FEATHER
P.O. Box 96
Bruceton Mills, West Va.
  Send your want list.

FORD PARTS OBSOLETE
616 East Florence
Los Angeles 1, Calif.
  Send your want list.

GAYLE AUTO PARTS
1019 McKee Street
Houston, Texas

SHORTY GIBSON'S
Rt. #8
Marysville, Tenn.
  Large Stock. Send your want list.

CHUCK HAFNER
Speedometer Service Company
4740 Baum Boulevard
Pittsburgh 13, Pa.
  Speedometers and parts.

BILL HALL
P.O. Box 615
Zanesville, Ohio

FRANK HANKINS
Route 25, R.D.
Riverside, N.J.

JOHN HANSEN
350 Paderewski Avenue
Perth Amboy, N.J.
  New hub caps.

J. L. HELMS, JR.
3912 Plaza Street
Charlotte, N.C.
  Manufactures new running boards, trim, etc.

E. R. HEMMINGS
P.O. Box 433A
Quincy, Illinois.
  Large Stock. Parts list available.

RAY HOVE
5606 Clinton Avenue
Minneapolis, Minn.

RICHARD G. HUBER
See MARK Auto Co.

JIM'S SOHIO SERVICE
1131 Cleveland Avenue
Ashland, Ohio.

JUDSON MANUFACTURING COMPANY, INC.
Cornwells Heights, Penn.
  Manufacturer of aluminum pistons.

DONALD KAUFMAN
97 Appleton Avenue
Pittsfield, Mass.

NORMAN KAYE
45 Chamberlin Drive
Buffalo 10, N.Y.

DALE KILBORNE
4703 Hersholt Avenue
Long Beach 8, Calif.
  Aluminum FORD runningboard step plates.

CHARLES KLINGER
114 South Mountain Avenue
Montclair, N.J.

LEO'S MODEL T REPAIR
911 East 18th Street
Kansas City 8, Missouri.
  Also supplies MODEL A parts.

RICHARD LA SALLE
(See MODEL A FORD parts & service).

J. S. MAPLES
4122 - 5th Avenue, South
Birmingham, Alabama.
  Send your want list.

MARK AUTO COMPANY, INC.
Layton, New Jersey

PAUL MARVEL
62 Spencer Avenue
Lancaster, Pa.
  Speedomter parts & service.

MIDWEST CLASSIC & ANTIQUE CARS & PARTS
(Ray Butler & Bobb Tapp)
1837 California
Denver 2, Colorado
  Send your want list.

JOE McCLELLAND
See FORD PARTS OBSOLETE

McKENQUIE MOTOR SALES
109 Broadway Street
Cambridge, Mass.
  Send your want list.

MODEL A FORD PARTS & SERVICE
(Richard La Salle)
907 Sterner Mill Road
Trevose, Bucks Co., Pa.
  Send your want list.

MURCHIO'S MOTOR CAR MUSEUM
(Joseph J. Murchio)
Greenwood Lake, N.Y.

JOE OSTERMAN
Box 234
Sugarcreek, Ohio
   Original type mufflers.

PARKINSON MOTOR SALES
Ponca City, Oklahoma.
   Send your want list.

R. N. PEDRICK
131 Kent Avenue
Kentfield, Calif.
   Original type motometers.

GENE RENNINGER
123 Lincoln Street
Lancaster, Pa.
   Large Stock.

ED. P. RYAN
530 Broadway
Malden 48, Mass.
   Send your want list.

G. S. SCHULZE
1207 South 91st
West Allis, Wis.
   Send your want list.

REID SHAW
2009 Edgewood Avenue
High Point, N.C.
   Send your want list.

K. L. SLINGERLAND
Cherry Ridge Farms
Westtown, N.Y.

HARRY R. SMITH
81-35 Margaret Place
Glendale, N.Y.

OLLIE L. SMITH
304 Jerome Avenue
Linthicum, Maryland

DALE STOCKMAN
R & F Mfg. Co.
Box 166
Bourbon, Indiana.
   Original type wind wing brackets.

AL VIVIAN ANTIQUE AUTO PARTS
156 - J Street
San Bernardino, Calif.
   Send your want list.

WARSHAWSKY & COMPANY
1900 - 24 South State Street
Chicago 16, Illinois.
   Original type mufflers.

CHARLES WENDLING
Frankfort, Kansas

J. R. WEATHERLY, JR.
Rt. #2, Box 5
Crossett, Arkansas

B. S. WISNIEWSKI, INC.
201-245 West Maple St.
Milwaukee 4, Wisconsin

JAMES A. WOLFRAM
2845 - 40th Avenue
Minneapolis 6, Minn.
   Chassis & body parts; send your want list.

ED. WRIGHT
876 Bay Street
Springfield, Mass.
   Send your want list.

3. POPULAR MAIL ORDER HOUSE CATALOG LISTINGS

Three popular mail order houses still offer a large selection of MODEL A Ford parts: Sears Roebuck & Company, Philadelphia, Pa.; Montgomery Ward & Co., Baltimore, Md.; and J. C. Whitney & Company, 1917 Archer, Chicago, Ill. Even the MODEL A restorers who are familiar with these sources often miss some of the items offered because they are buried amid the multitude of parts for modern cars. Here, then, is a handy compilation of parts available in 1958 for MODEL A Fords:

MODEL A FORD PARTS

FRONT WHEEL BEARING—1928-48
   One Front Wheel Set   Sears 28D4192 $ 4.95   1 - 8
      (includes grease retainer) Wards 61C2611 $ 4.95   2 - 0
REAR WHEEL BEARING—1928-36
   One Rear Wheel Set   Wards 61C2615 $ 1.55   1 - 0
GREASE RETAINERS—1928-38
   Rear Wheel, outer, pair   Sears 28D3837 $ .95   0 - 6
                               Wards 61C2304 $ .98   0 - 6
   Rear Wheel, inner, pair   Sears 28D3838 $ .75   0 - 6
DIFFERENTIAL ASSEMBLY—1928-31 (No exchange)
   Rebuilt; completely assembled
   in center housing; new ring and
   pinion bearings, etc. Specify
   Model A Ford.   Whitney A5136 $20.95
UNIVERSAL JOINT—1928-48
   Universal Joint   Sears 28D4781 $ 3.59   3 - 10
                               Wards 61C2509 $ 3.75   4 - 0
                               Whitney 84235 $ 4.59
RADIATOR
   1928-29 Radiator   Sears 28D09305L $28.95   25 - 0
                               Wards 61C4800M0 $31.50   20 - 0
                               Whitney 72056 $35.95
   1930-31 Radiator   Sears 28D09312L $29.95   23 - 0
                               Wards 61C4801M0 $32.45   20 - 0
                               Whitney 72057 $39.65
WATER PUMP—1928-31
   Complete Pump, roller brg. Sears 28D4769 $ 3.59   4 - 0
                               Whitney 36117 $ 4.95
WATER PUMP REPAIR KIT—1928-31
   Kit   Wards 61C1996 $ 1.59   2 - 0
FAN BELT—1928-31
   Model A Ford Fan Belt   Sears 28D2828 $ .89   0 - 14
                               Whitney 73000 $ .85
TIMING GEAR—1928-34
   Standard size, Bakelite   Sears 28D2535 $ 1.98   0 - 11
                               Whitney 32810 $ 2.11
   .003" oversize, Bakelite   Wards 61C2221 $ 1.67   2 - 2
   .004" oversize, Bakelite   Sears 28D2551 $ 2.19   0 - 12
ENGINE VALVE SPRINGS—1928-34
   Set of 8   Sears 28D3202 $ 1.19   0 - 12
                               Wards 61C300 $ 1.25   2 - 0
ENGINE VALVES—1928-32
   Intake Valves   Sears 28D2940 $ .69 ea. 0 - 5
                               Wards 61C411 $ 3.15 set 2 - 0
   Exhaust Valves   Sears 28D3040 $ .69 ea. 0 - 5
                               Wards 61C411 $ 3.15 set 2 - 0
ENGINE VALVE GUIDES—1928-32
   Valve Guides, set of 8   Sears 28D4741 $ 1.98 set 1 - 8
                               Wards 61C357 $ .25 ea. 0 - 4
PISTONS—1928-34 (Including Pins) State: Std., .020, .030, .040, .060 oversize.
   Set of 4, Reg. 3 ring type Sears 28D3507F $ 9.95 set 8 - 0
   Reg. 3-ring type, aluminum Whitney 33100 $ 3.35 ea.
   Set of 4, Spl. 4 ring type Sears 28D3518F $10.50 set 8 - 0
PISTON PINS—1928-34—State: Std., .003, .005 oversize.
   Set of 4 Piston Pins   Sears 28D3408 $ 2.59 set 3 - 0
PISTON RINGS—1928-34—State: Std., .020, .030, .040, .060 oversize.
   "Steel Master" 3-Ring Piston Sears 28D3650 $ 3.49 set 1 - 8
   "Chrome Master" 3-Ring
     Piston   Sears 28D3611 $ 3.98 set 1 - 8
   "Super Chromeoil" 3-Ring
     Piston   Wards 61C714K $ 4.75 set 2 - 0
   "Chromeoil" 3-Ring Piston   Wards 61C514K $ 4.25 set 2 - 0
   "Flexible" 3-Ring Piston   Wards 61C565K $ 2.95 set 2 - 0
   "Top Quality" 3-Ring Piston Whitney 33307 $ 2.10 set
   "Steel Master" 4-Ring Piston Sears 28D3661F $ 4.29 set 1 - 8
   "Chrome Master" 4-Ring
     Piston   Sears 28D3612F $ 5.45 set 1 - 8
   "Top Quality" 4-Ring Piston Whitney 33308 $ 2.69 set

SPARK COIL—1928-34
   Model A Ford Coil   Wards 61C1179 $ 3.25   3 - 0
                                      Whitney 45921 $ 2.85
   Universal Type Coil   Sears 28D8213 $ 2.98   2 - 3

DISTRIBUTOR TUNE-UP KIT—1928-31 (Incl. points, rotor, condenser)
   Distributor Kit   Sears 28D8290 $ .77   0 - 8
                                      Wards 61C1109 $ .75   0 - 4

DISTRIBUTOR PARTS—1928-31
   Body and Cover   Wards 61C1227 $ .89   0 - 13
   Body only   Whitney 45481 $ .76
   Cover only   Whitney 45482 $ .25
   Rotor only   Whitney 45451 $ .15
   Points only   Whitney 45525 $ .27
   Cam only   Whitney 45281 $ .64

SPARK PLUGS—Size 7/8" SAE
   Model A Ford Spark Plugs Sears 28D201 $ .53 ea. 0 - 4
   Model A Ford Spark Plugs Wards 61C1585 $ .55 ea. 0 - 6
     Set of 4 or more   Sears 28D201 $ .47 ea. 0 - 4
     Set of 4 or more   Wards 61C1585 $ .49 ea. 0 - 6

ENGINE GASKETS—1928-31
   Complete Overhaul Set   Sears 28D4200 $ 3.59   2 - 0
                                      Wards 61C2102L $ 4.62   2 - 0
                                      Whitney 34323 $ 4.79
   Head Gasket only   Sears 28D4040 $ 1.79   2 - 0
                                      Wards 61C2047L $ 2.31   2 - 0
                                      Whitney 34323 $ 4.79
   Manifold only   Sears 28D4082 $ .25   0 - 8
                                      Wards 61C2181 $ .25   0 - 8
                                      Whitney 34031 $ .39
   Valve Grinding Set   Sears 28D4264 $ 2.49   1 - 0
                                      Wards 61C2008L $ 3.28   1 - 8
   Oil Pan Set   Sears 28D4001 $ .79   2 - 0
                                      Wards 61C2128L $ .45   1 - 7
                                      Whitney 34211 $ .89

SHEET CORK GASKET MATERIAL
   12"x 36"x 1/16"   Sears 28D3999 $ .49   0 - 8
                                      Wards 61C2162 $ .49   0 - 6
   12"x 36"x 1/8"   Sears 28D4006 $ .99   0 - 13
                                      Wards 61C2163 $ .98   0 - 12

KING BOLT SET—1928-31
   King Bolt and Bushings   Sears 28D4344 $ 3.45   2 - 8
                                      Wards 61C4213 $ 3.45   3 - 0
                                      Whitney 83215 $ 4.35

KING BOLT REAMER—1928-31
   Reamer   Wards 61C9360 $ 1.93   1 - 0

TIE ROD ENDS (Pair)—1928-34
   Tie Rod Ends, pair   Sears 28D2617 $ 3.95   3 - 6

STEERING GEAR SECTOR SET—1929-31
   2-Tooth Sector Set   Wards 61C4351 $ 2.95   3 - 12

BRAKE LINING SET—1928-31 (Incl. rivets)
   Brake Lining Set   Sears 28D1975 $ 2.75   2 - 14
                                      Wards 61C2779 $ 2.89   1 - 4
                                      Whitney 85159 $ 3.50

BRAKE LINING RIVETING TOOL
   Riveting Tool   Sears 28D1933 $ .95   1 - 4
                                      Wards 61C9438 $ 1.29   1 - 4

FRONT SPRING—1928-31
   Front Spring   Sears 28D09729K $ 9.29   22 - 0
                                      Whitney 82317 $19.98

SPRING SHACKLES—1928-31
   Front Spring Shackles   Sears 28D4755 $ 1.85   3 - 8
                                      Wards 61C3500 $ 1.59   2 - 0
   Rear Spring Shackles   Wards 61C3501 $ 1.79   2 - 0

SHOCK ABSORBER LINKS—1928-32
   Links with Rubber Cushions Sears 28D4706 $ .79 ea. 0 - 13

MUFFLER—1928-32
   Replacement Type Muffler   Sears 28D08613L $ 5.79 ea. 11 - 0
                                      Whitney 23301 $ 7.15

GENERATOR—1928-32
   Rebuilt Generator (no exch.) Wards 61C1455M $ 7.95   22 - 0

STARTER—1928-32
   Rebuilt Starter (no exchange) Wards 61C1302M $ 7.98   22 - 0
   Rebuilt Starter (no exchange) Whitney 47123 $10.45

STARTER DRIVE ASSEMBLY—1929-54
   Starter Drive Assembly   Wards 61C1396 $ 2.69   1 - 12
   Rebuilt Starter Drive Ass'y   Whitney 45703 $ 1.79

TRANSMISSION—1929-31
   Rebuilt Transmission
     (no exchange)   Wards 61C3733M0 $44.95   40 - 0
                                      Whitney T4310 $25.50

CLUTCH PRESSURE PLATE AND DISC SET—1929-34
   Clutch Set   Sears 28D03250 $11.95   20 - 0

CLUTCH DISC—1929-34
   Clutch Disc, 1929-34   Sears 28D4108 $ 4.19   4 - 0
   Clutch Disc, only   Whitney 81213 $ 5.30

CLUTCH THROW-OUT BEARING—1929-48
   Clutch Release Bearing   Sears 28D5399 $ 1.98   1 - 1
                                      Wards 61C2400 $ 2.65   2 - 0

GENERATOR CUT-OUT—1928-32
   Generator Cut-out   Wards 61C1434 $ .79   1 - 0

CARBURETOR REPAIR KIT—1928-31
   Zenith Repair Kit   Wards 61C1825 $ 1.19   0 - 8

CARBURETOR—1928-31
   New Tillotson Replacement Wards 61C1620 $ 7.75   5 - 0

SHOCK ABSORBERS—Rebuilt, not exchange, 1928-31
   Front pair   Whitney 87116 $ 9.95 pr.
   Rear pair   Whitney 87117 $ 9.95 pr.

CYLINDER HEADS
   Resurfaced, excellent condition Whitney C3789 $14.00

FLOOR MAT
   1928-31 Model A, felt backed
   black rubber, good quality. Whitney 12100 $ 3.98

RUNNING BOARD MATTING
   Black ribbed rubber, 13" wide Whitney 12070 $ .22 per foot

REBUILT ENGINES
   See catalogs for details   Sears 28HM4895F
    (no head, pan, pump)   Full price $139.95
                                      Exchange $119.95
                                    Whitney M1315
                                    Full price $139.50
                                    Exchange $129.50

TIRES AND TUBES
   Tire 4.50 x 21   Sears 95D02306 $14.70   17 - 0
                                      Wards 64C1542M $13.87   15 - 0
   Tube 4.50 x 21   Sears 95D8569 $ 2.30   4 - 0
                                      Wards 64C2701M $ 2.25   3 - 0
   Tire 4.74x19   Sears 95H02377 $15.25   18-0
                                      Wards 64A1543M $14.35   15-0
   Tube 4.75x19   Sears 95H8568 $ 2.70   3-0
                                      Wards 64A2703M $ 2.25   3-0

FIGURE 86 A

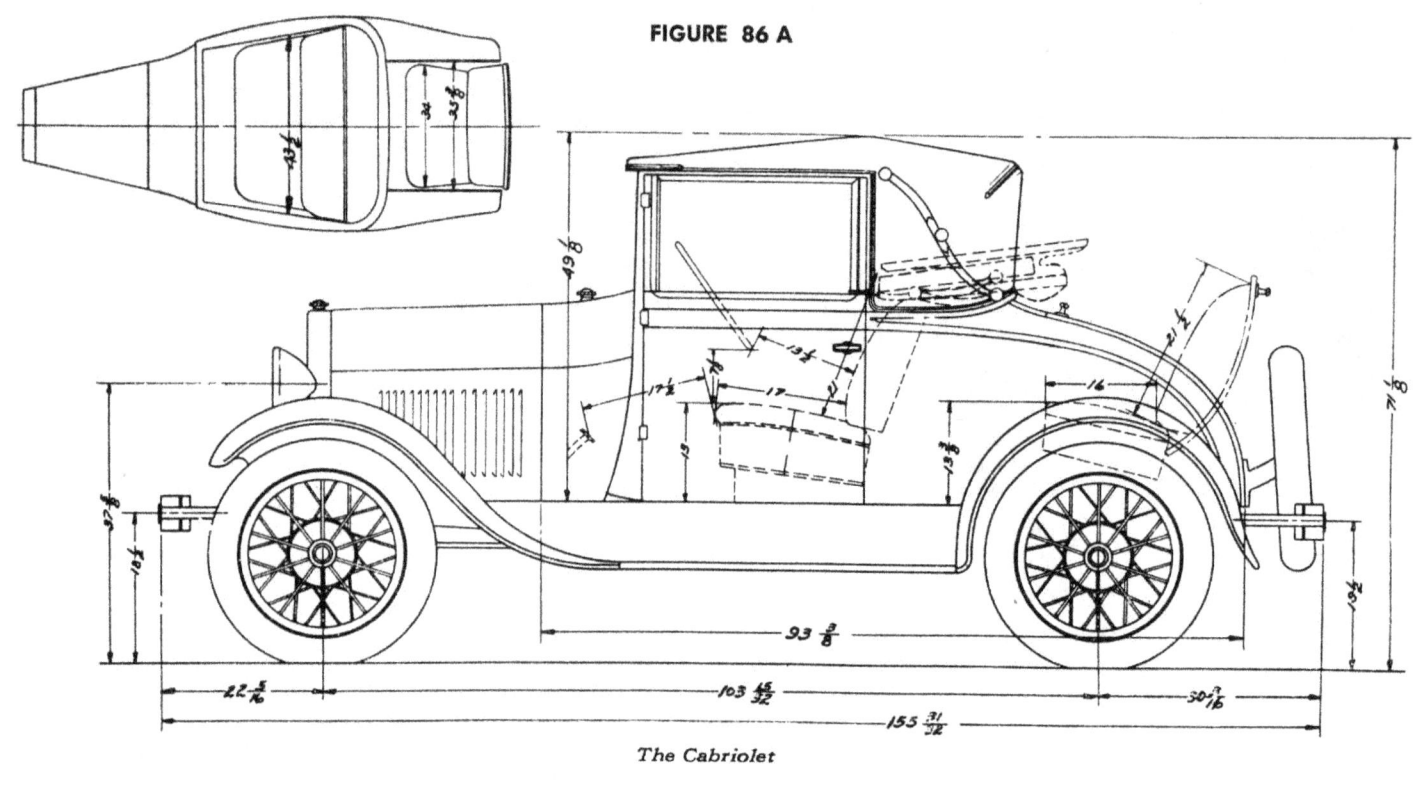

The Cabriolet

1929

FIGURE 86 B

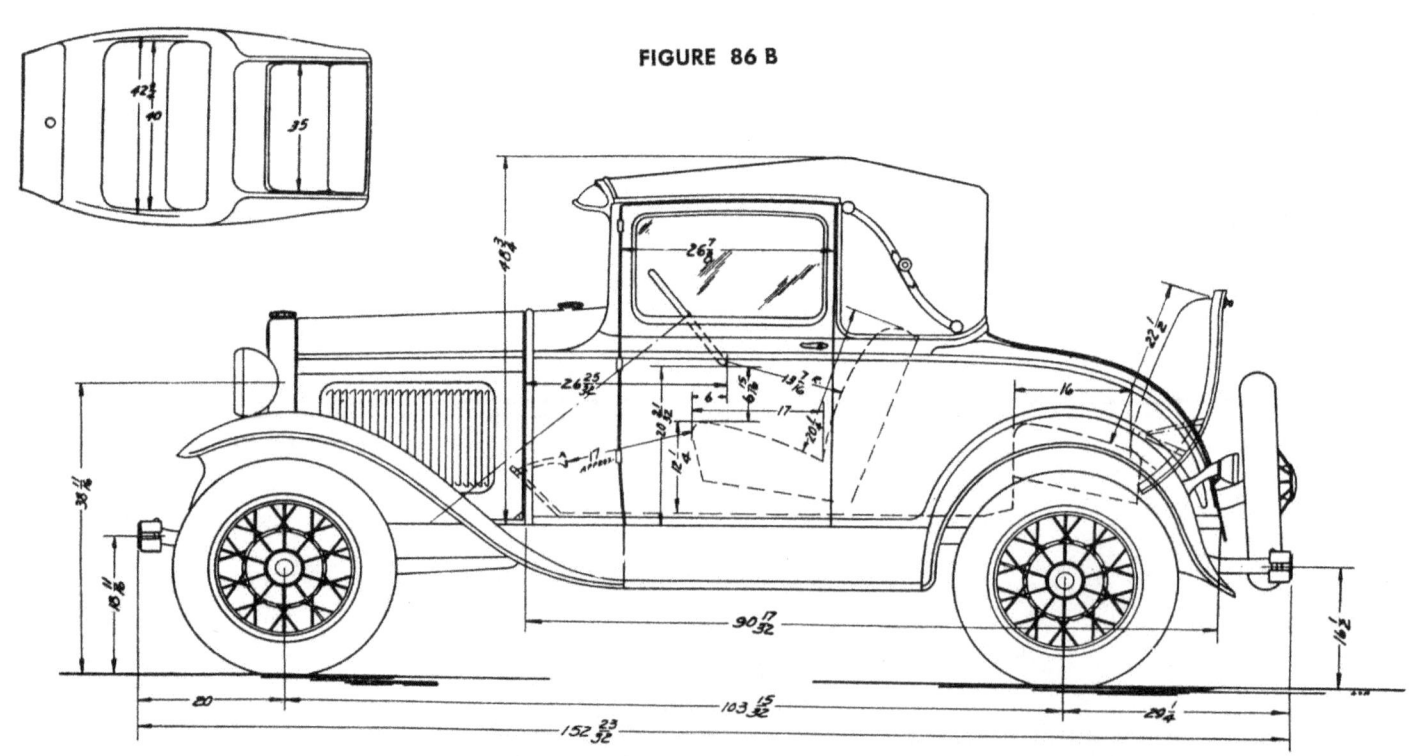

The Sport Coupe
(Dimensions approximately same for Cabriolet)

1930

FIGURE 87 A

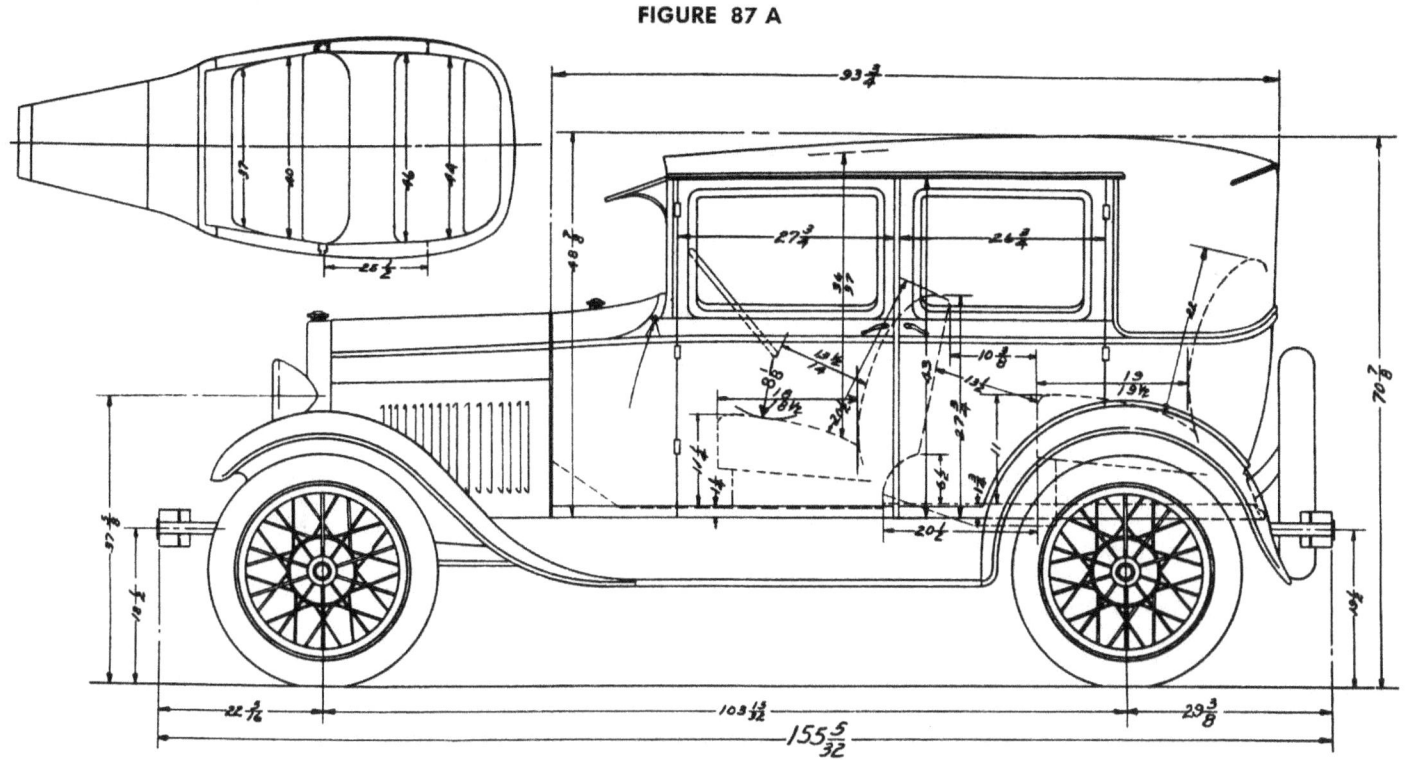

The Fordor Sedan

1929

FIGURE 87 B

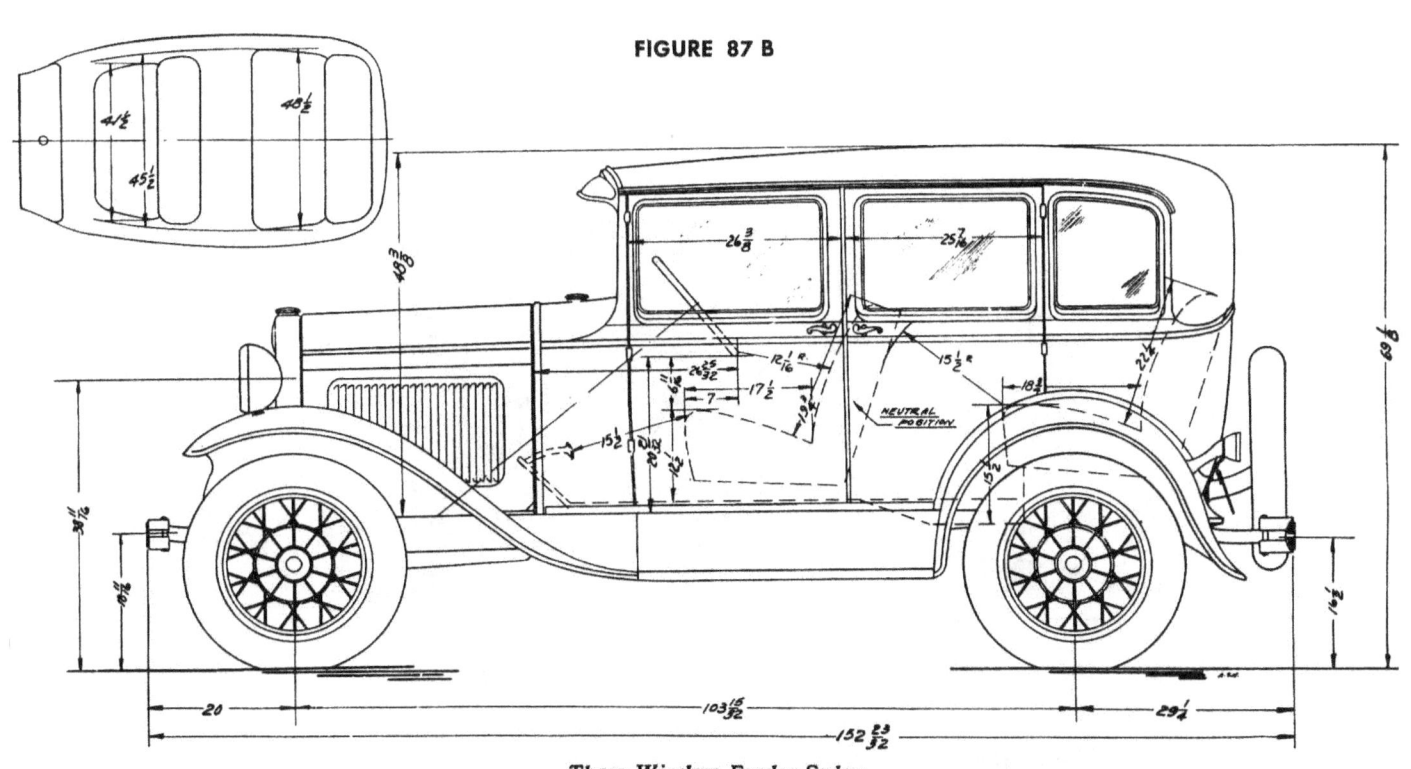

Three-Window Fordor Sedan
(Dimensions same for De Luxe Sedan)

1930

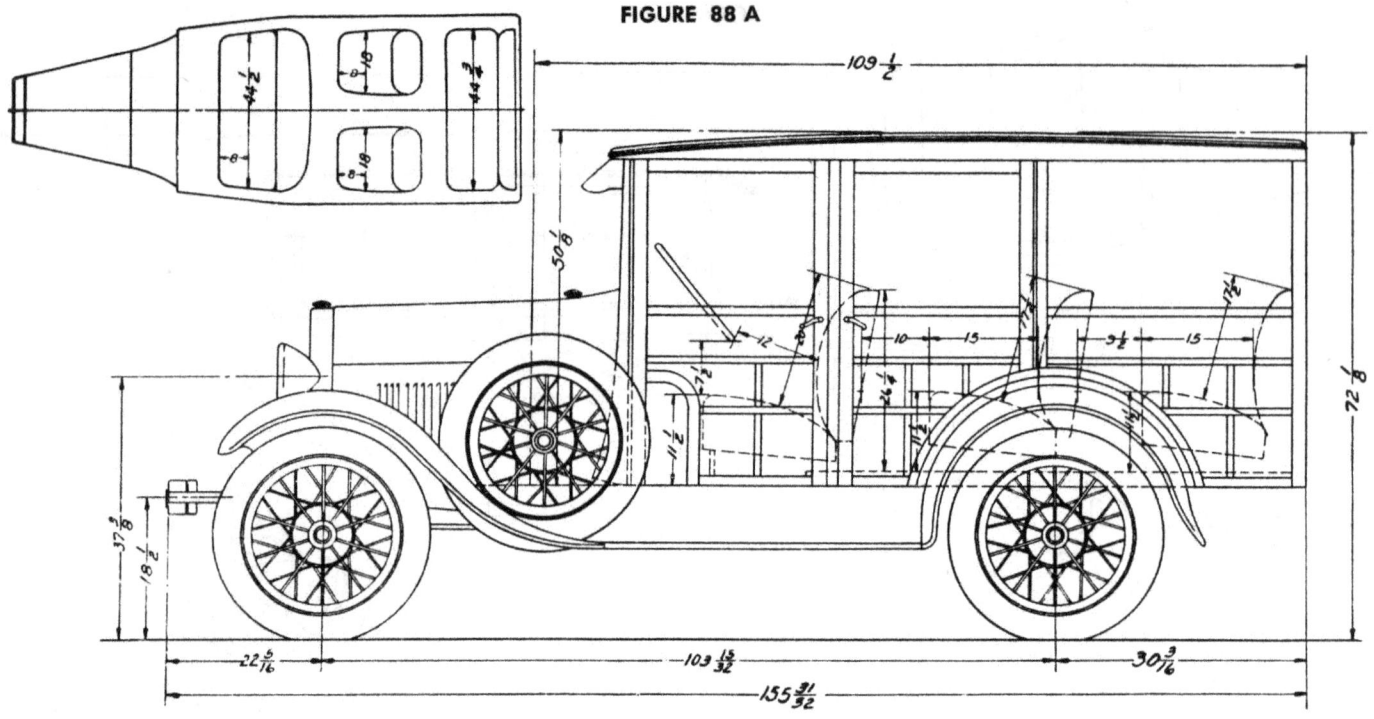

The Station Wagon

1929

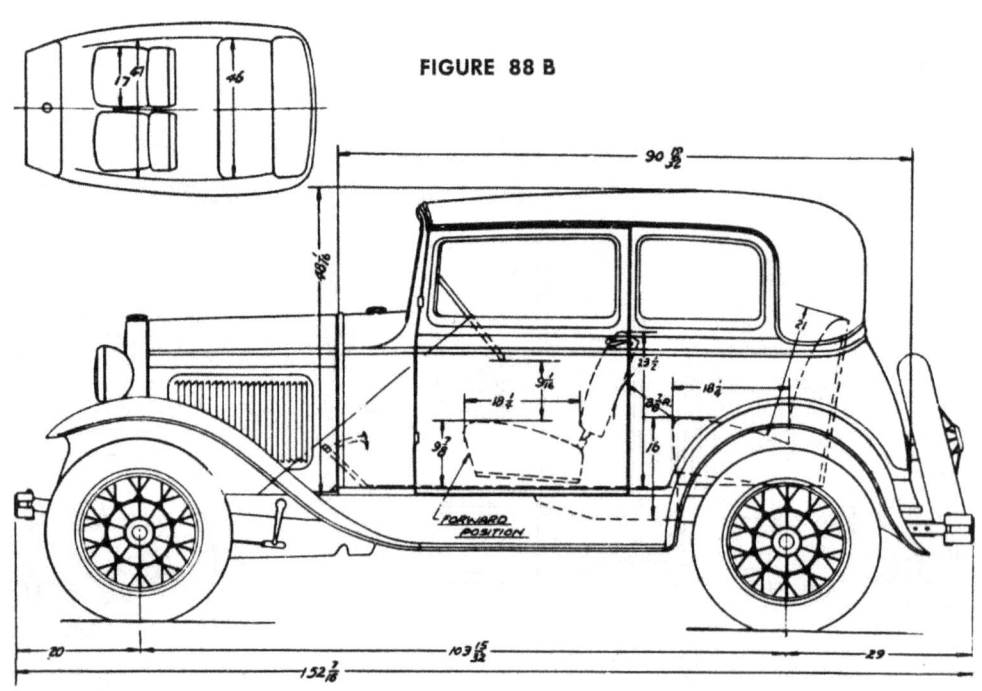

VICTORIA
(Dimensions approximately same for De Luxe Phaeton, except it is
3 inches longer from back of front seat)

1931

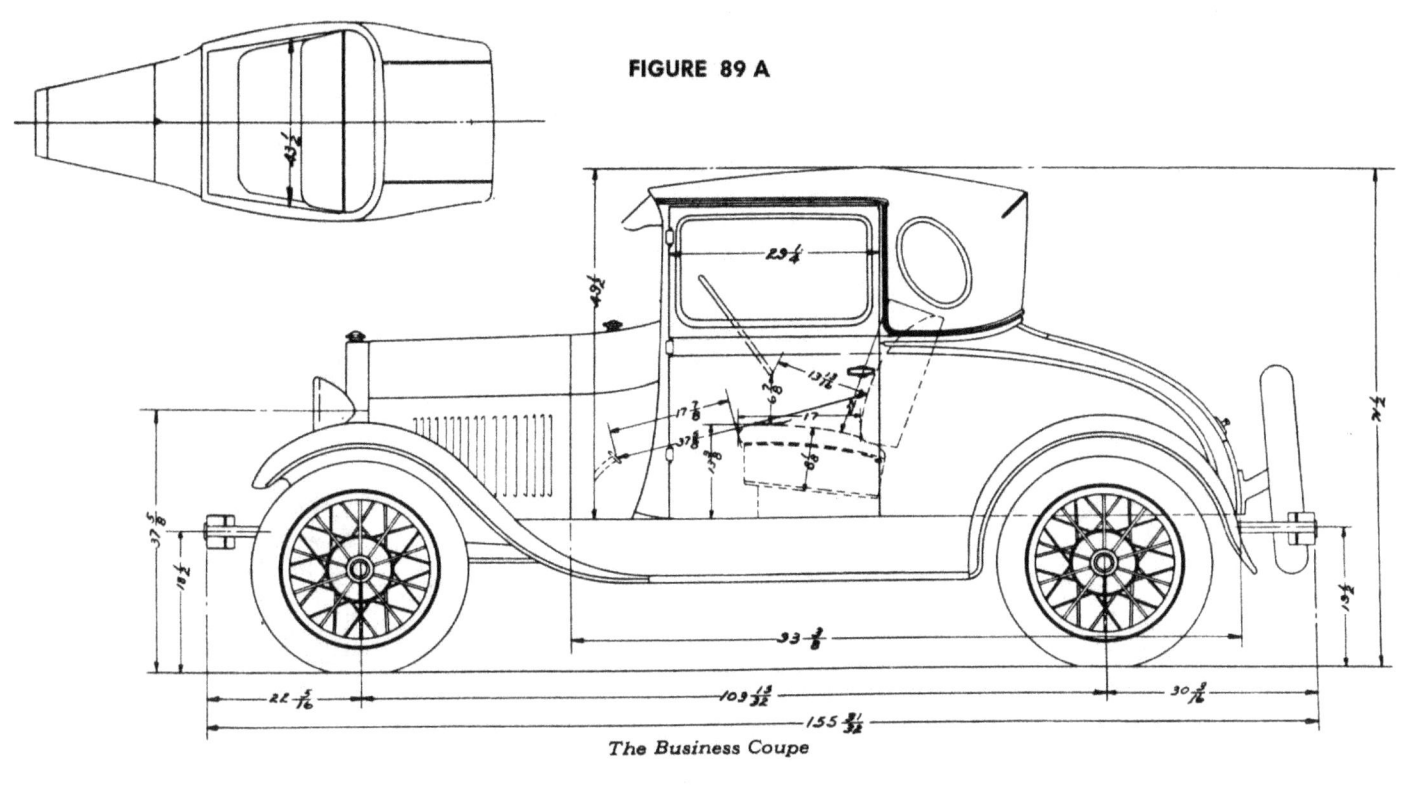

1929

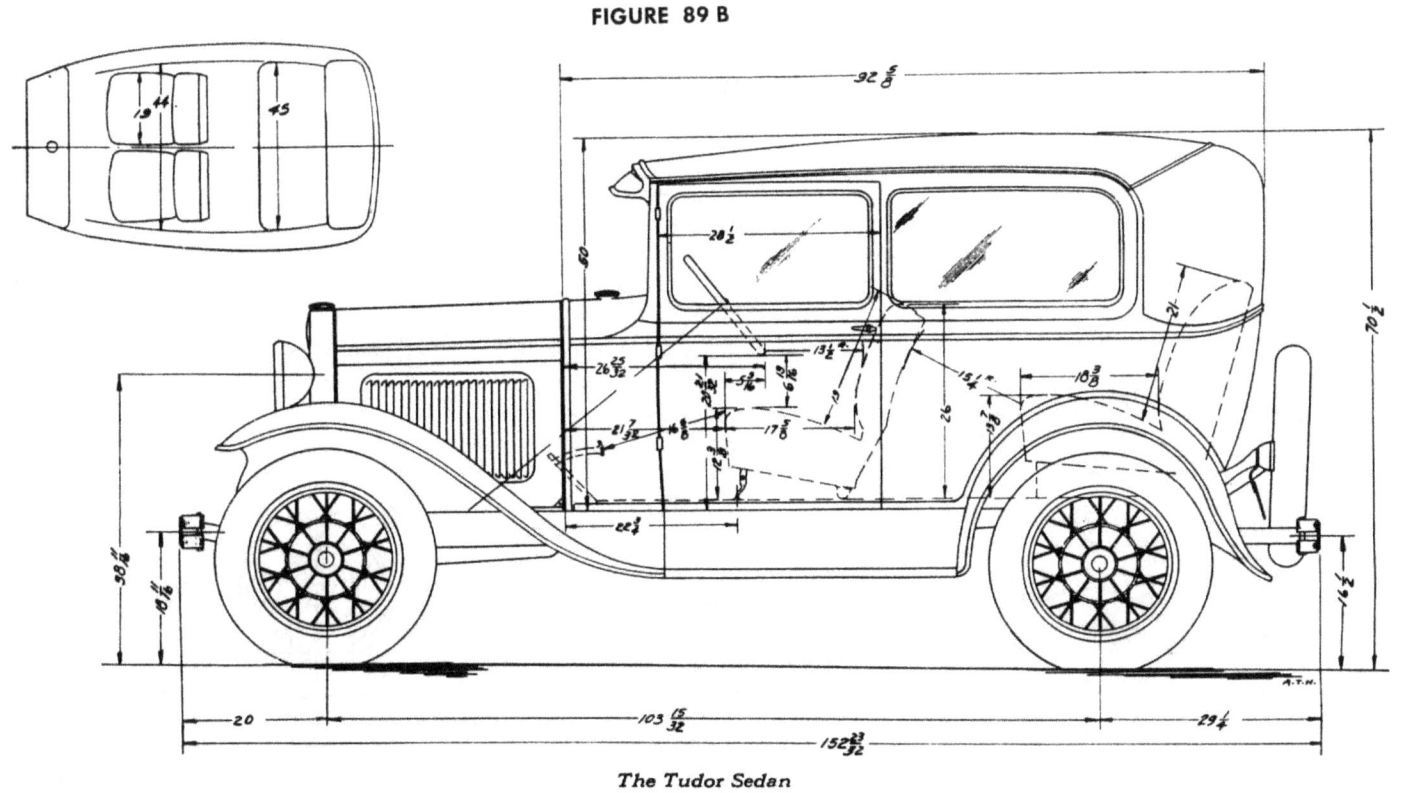

1930

105

FIGURE 90 A

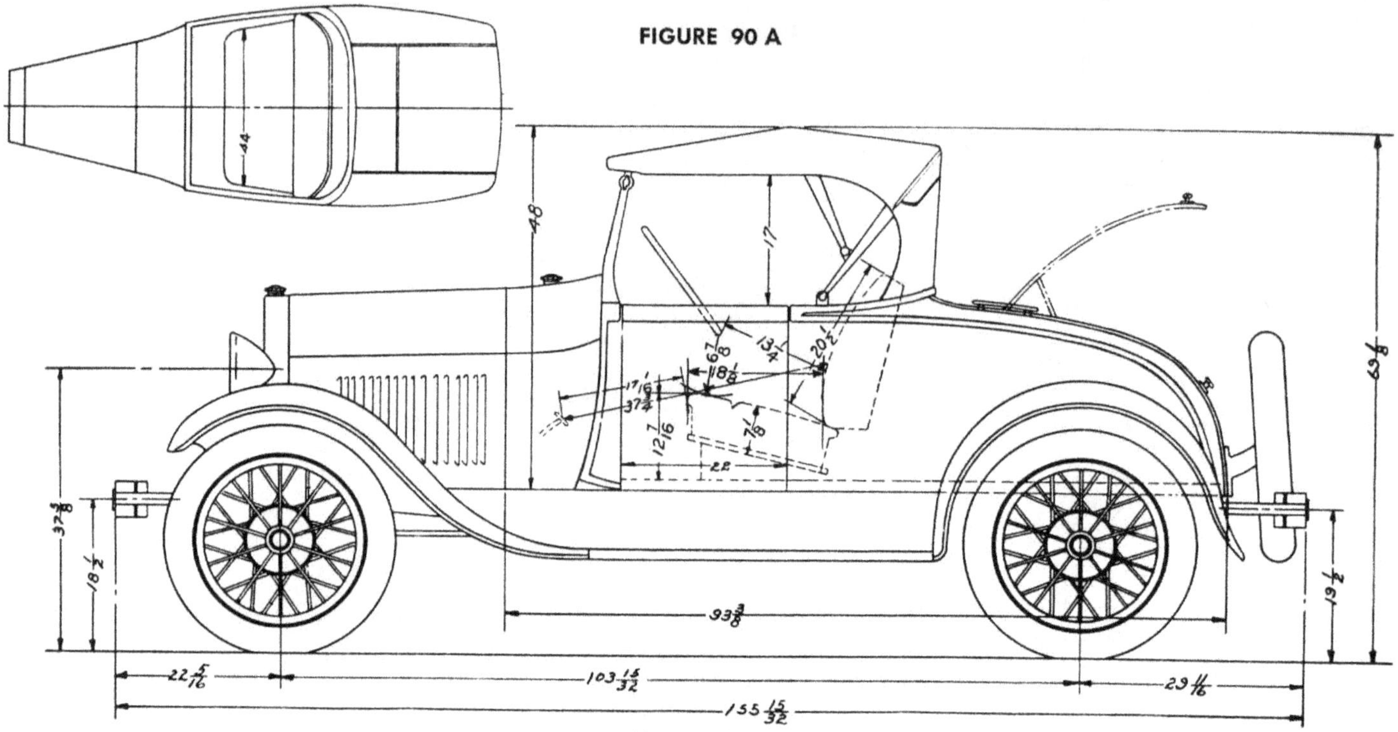

The Roadster

1929

FIGURE 90 B

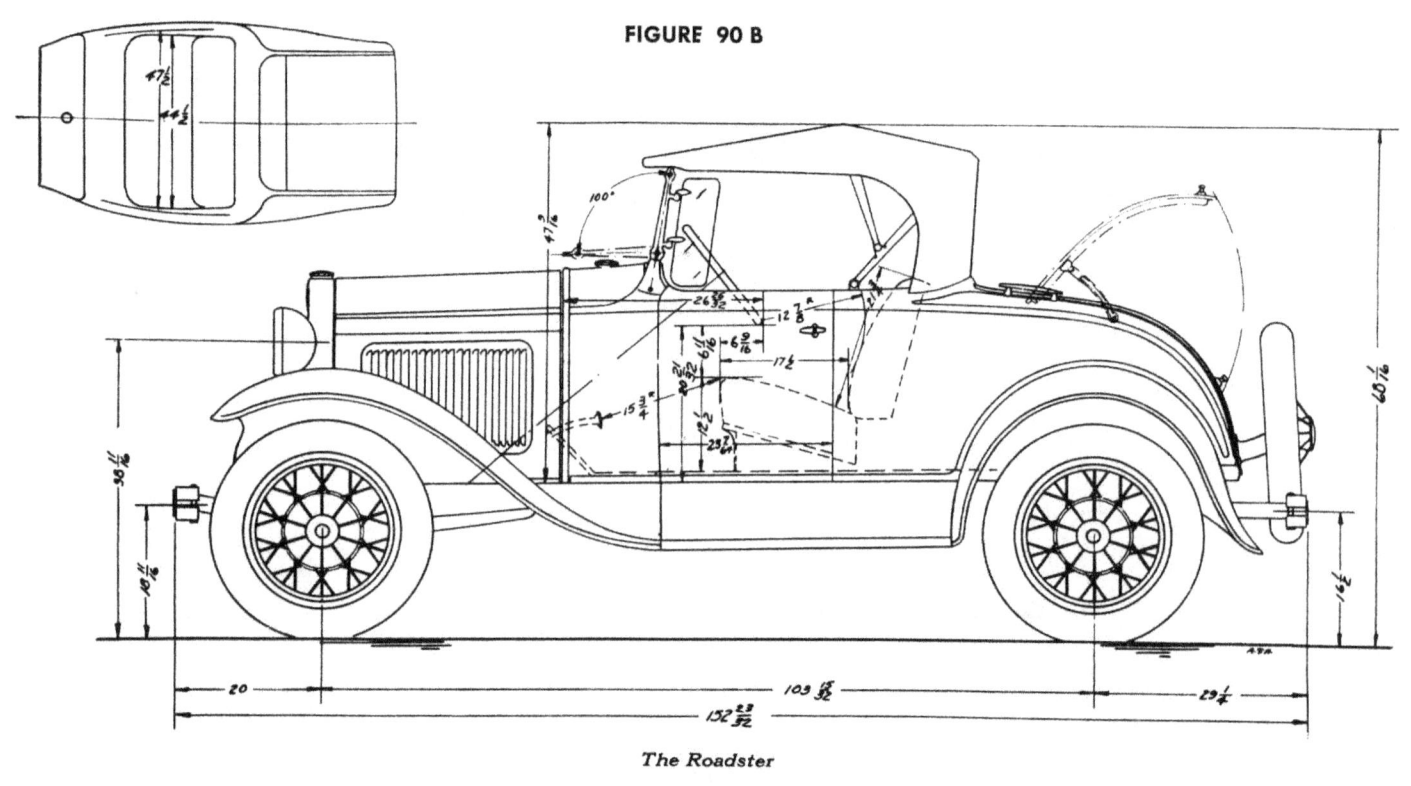

The Roadster

1930

Photo courtesy Ford Motor Company.

FIGURE 91. 1931 FORD VICTORIA COUPE.

Aristocratic in appearance, this Victoria coupe has seating for five passengers and luggage space in the "bustle" behind the rear seat. The roof is lower than other MODEL A cars and the floor is deeply recessed to provide interior head room. Upholstering is in dark brown mohair or broadcloth. Cowl lamps are regular equipment as is the vacuum windshield wiper motor. Note the one-piece splash apron characteristic of the 1931 Fords.

Photo courtesy Ford Motor Company.

FIGURE 92. 1931 FORD CABRIOLET (Convertible).

A sport car suitable for every season, this Cabriolet, 68-C, resembles the sport coupe when the top is raised. The interior upholstering is either tan Bedford cord or genuine crushed grain leather; the rumble seat is two-tone cross grain artificial leather.

Photo courtesy Ford Motor Company.

FIGURE 93. 1930 DE LUXE FORDOR SEDAN.

Sparkling colors and rich appointments bring to this sedan a truly de luxe atmosphere. Body type number 170-B was built by the Briggs Body Company. Upholstering is in either deep tan Bedford cord or in brown mohair.

Photo courtesy Ford Motor Company.

FIGURE 94. 1930 FORD TOWN SEDAN.

Cowl lamps are the external marks differentiating this town sedan (155-C or-D) from the Fordor sedan (165-C, -D or 170-B). The more luxurious interior is upholstered in Bedford cord or mohair, is fitted with hand loops on the door posts, and has comfortable arm rests at the sides and a center pull-down arm rest in rear cushion. The town sedan was often ordered and delivered with twin side-mounted spare wheels.

FIGURE 95 A   INTRODUCED IN 1927, Ford Model A two-door sedan had price tag of $495.

FIGURE 95 B   TOWN SEDAN OF 1931 kept same lines as 1927 model, was last Model A made.

FIGURE 95 C   ROADSTER OF 1931 had more chrome than earlier models and sleeker lines.

FIGURE 95 D   CONVERTIBLE TOURING model was popular for sporty lines and convenience.

1931 Ford 1½ Ton Panel Truck, 85-B.

DE LUXE POLICE PATROL

The De Luxe Police Patrol is designed to give long and reliable service under every condition. The sweeping lines and well-balanced proportions of this body make it pleasing in appearance, while its excellent finish and the evident care with which it was planned throughout add to its substantial value. The body is of steel, with composition interior trim. The opening at the rear is provided with a heavy curtain and with hand-rails at either side. There is a single step at the rear. Two long seats of plywood construction run the length of the rear compartment. These seats are hinged, and underneath each is a compartment of ample size for carrying a stretcher and necessary supplies. Between the front and rear compartments is a strong partition with a window protected by a wire screen. Equipment includes a buzzer for signalling the driver, a dome light in the rear compartment, a gun compartment just above the windshield, and a compartment over the partition for first-aid supplies.

Dimensions: Length, 102"; height, 61"; width, 54". Wheelbase, 131½".

TOWN CAR DELIVERY

This is a medium-sized body of distinctive appearance, unusual not only in its design, but in the completeness of its appointments and finish. Its sturdy construction adapts it for continued use as a delivery unit, while its striking but conservative good looks make it a favored choice with the exclusive retail shop for deliveries in city and suburbs. The outside of the body is all aluminum. The inside consists of a strong wooden frame, covered with veneer panels finished in natural color. Connecting the driver's compartment with the loading compartment is a full length sliding door. The driver's seat is deeply cushioned, and is upholstered in black genuine leather. The equipment includes an ornamental light on either side of the body, an extension mirror on the left side, fender-well in left front fender, and five steel spoke wheels, slanting windshield that contributes to smart appearance, and a special canopy to cover the driver's compartment during inclement weather. There is a wide choice of colors.

Body dimensions: Length, 46"; width, 43½"; height, 42". Wheelbase, 103½".

1931 VICTORIA COUPE   190-A

This rear three-quarter view of the Victoria reveals its simple, classically beautiful lines and displays the gracefulness of the bustle-backed body, accentuated by the rakish angle of the windshield in front and the spare tire in the back. Separate front seats tip foreward to provide access to the rear through the wide door. More familiar with the steel top, this Victoria with the Tan fabric-covered top is an attractive variation. Cowl lamps are regular equipment.

ARE YOU:
INTERESTED IN EUROPEAN, IMPORT & EXOTIC AUTOMOBILES?

DO YOU:
DO YOUR OWN MAINTENANCE?

If you answered yes to either of these questions, then you should check out our automobile books and manuals. We have included a sample listing of some of our featured marques. However, for complete details and the most up-to-date information, please visit our website.

—— www.VelocePress.com ——

The fastest growing specialist USA publisher of niche market automotive books and manuals.

All VelocePress titles are available through your local independent bookseller, Amazon.com or direct from VelocePress. Wholesale customers may also purchase direct or from the Ingram Book Group.

AUTOBOOKS WORKSHOP MANUALS

ALFA ROMEO GIULIA 1300, 1600, 1750, 2000 1962-1978 WSM
AUSTIN HEALEY SPRITE, MG MIDGET 1958-1980 WSM
BMW 1600 1966-1973 WSM
BMW 2000 & 2002 1966-1976 WSM
BMW 2500, 2800, 3.0 & 3.3 1968-1977 WSM
BMW 316, 320, 320i 1975-1977 WSM
BMW 518, 520, 520i 1973-1981 WSM
FIAT 1100, 1100D, 1100R & 1200 1957-1969 WSM
FIAT 124 1966-1974 WSM
FIAT 124 SPORT 1966-1975 WSM
FIAT 125 & 125 SPECIAL 1967-1973 WSM
FIAT 126, 126L, 126 DV, 126/650 & 126/650 DV 1972-1982 WSM
FIAT 127 SALOON, SPECIAL & SPORT, 900, 1050 1971-1981 WSM
FIAT 128 1969-1982 WSM
FIAT 1300, 1500 1961-1967 WSM
FIAT 131 MIRAFIORI 1975-1982 WSM
FIAT 132 1972-1982 WSM
FIAT 500 1957-1973 WSM
FIAT 600, 600D & MULTIPLA 1955-1969 WSM
FIAT 850 1964-1972 WSM
JAGUAR E-TYPE 1961-1972 WSM
JAGUAR MK 1, 2 1955-1969 WSM
JAGUAR S TYPE, 420 1963-1968 WSM
JAGUAR XK 120, 140, 150 MK 7, 8, 9 1948-1961 WSM
LAND ROVER 1, 2 1948-1961 WSM
MERCEDES-BENZ 190 1959-1968 WSM
MERCEDES-BENZ 220/8 1968-1972 WSM
MERCEDES-BENZ 220B 1959-1965 WSM
MERCEDES-BENZ 230 1963-1968 WSM
MERCEDES-BENZ 250 1968-1972 WSM
MERCEDES-BENZ 280 1968-1972 WSM
MG MIDGET TA-TF 1936-1955 WSM
MINI 1959-1980 WSM
MORRIS MINOR 1952-1971 WSM
PEUGEOT 404 1960-1975 WSM
PORSCHE 911 1964-1973 WSM
PORSCHE 911 1970-1977 WSM
RENAULT 16 1965-1979 WSM
RENAULT 8, 10, 1100 1962-1971 WSM
ROVER 3500, 3500S 1968-1976 WSM
SUNBEAM RAPIER, ALPINE 1955-1965 WSM
TRIUMPH SPITFIRE, GT6, VITESSE 1962-1968 WSM
TRIUMPH TR2, TR3, TR3A 1952-1962 WSM
TRIUMPH TR4, TR4A 1961-1967 WSM
VOLKSWAGEN BEETLE 1968-1977 WSM

BROOKLANDS BOOKS & ROAD TEST PORTFOLIOS (RTP)

AC CARS 1904-2009
ALFA ROMEO 1920-1933 ROAD TEST PORTFOLIO
ALFA ROMEO 1934-1940 ROAD TEST PORTFOLIO
BRABHAM RALT HONDA THE RON TAURANAC STORY
BUGATTI TYPE 10 TO TYPE 40 ROAD TEST PORTFOLIO
BUGATTI TYPE 10 TO TYPE 251 ROAD TEST PORTFOLIO
BUGATTI TYPE 41 TO TYPE 55 ROAD TEST PORTFOLIO
BUGATTI TYPE 57 TO TYPE 251 ROAD TEST PORTFOLIO
DELAHAYE ROAD TEST PORTFOLIO
FERRARI ROAD CARS 1946-1956 ROAD TEST PORTFOLIO
FIAT 500 1936-1972 ROAD TEST PORTFOLIO
FIAT DINO ROAD TEST PORTFOLIO
HISPANO SUIZA ROAD TEST PORTFOLIO
HONDA ST1100/ST1300 PAN EUROPEAN 1990-2002 RTP
JAGUAR MK1 & MK2 ROAD TEST PORTFOLIO
LOTUS CORTINA ROAD TEST PORTFOLIO
MV AGUSTA F4 750 & 1000 1997-2007 ROAD TEST PORTFOLIO
TATRA CARS ROAD TEST PORTFOLIO

VELOCEPRESS AUTOMOBILE BOOKS & MANUALS

ABARTH BUYERS GUIDE
AUSTIN-HEALEY 6-CYLINDER WSM
BMW 600 LIMOUSINE FACTORY WSM
BMW 600 LIMOUSINE OWNERS HAND BOOK & SERVICE MANUAL
BMW ISETTA FACTORY WSM
BOOK OF THE CARRERA PANAMERICANA - MEXICAN ROAD RACE
COMPLETE CATALOG OF JAPANESE MOTOR VEHICLES
DIALED IN - THE JAN OPPERMAN STORY
FERRARI 250/GT SERVICE AND MAINTENANCE
FERRARI 308 SERIES BUYER'S AND OWNER'S GUIDE
FERRARI BERLINETTA LUSSO
FERRARI BROCHURES AND SALES LITERATURE 1946-1967
FERRARI BROCHURES AND SALES LITERATURE 1968-1989
FERRARI GUIDE TO PERFORMANCE
FERRARI OPP, MAINTENANCE & SERVICE H/BOOKS 1948-1963
FERRARI OWNER'S HANDBOOK
FERRARI SERIAL NUMBERS PART I - ODD NUMBERS TO 21399
FERRARI SERIAL NUMBERS PART II - EVEN NUMBERS TO 1050
FERRARI SPYDER CALIFORNIA
FERRARI TUNING TIPS & MAINTENANCE TECHNIQUES
HENRY'S FABULOUS MODEL "A" FORD
HOW TO BUILD A FIBERGLASS CAR
HOW TO BUILD A RACING CAR
IF HEMINGWAY HAD WRITTEN A RACING NOVEL
JAGUAR E-TYPE 3.8 & 4.2 WSM
LE MANS 24 (THE BOOK THAT THE FILM WAS BASED ON)
MASERATI BROCHURES AND SALES LITERATURE
MASERATI OWNER'S HANDBOOK
METROPOLITAN FACTORY WSM
MGA & MGB OWNERS HANDBOOK & WSM
OBERT'S FIAT GUIDE
PERFORMANCE TUNING THE SUNBEAM TIGER
PORSCHE 356 1948-1965 WSM
PORSCHE 912 WSM
SOUPING THE VOLKSWAGEN
TRIUMPH TR2, TR3, TR4 1953-1965 WSM
VEDA ORR'S NEW REVISED HOT ROD PICTORIAL
VOLKSWAGEN TRANSPORTER, TRUCKS, STATION WAGONS WSM
VOLVO 1944-1968 ALL MODELS WSM

VELOCEPRESS MOTORCYCLE BOOKS & MANUALS

AJS SINGLES 1955-65 350cc & 500cc (BOOK OF)
ARIEL 1939-1960 4 STROKE SINGLES (BOOK OF)
ARIEL LEADER & ARROW 1958-1964 (BOOK OF)
ARIEL MOTORCYCLES 1933-1951 WSM
ARIEL PREWAR MODELS 1932-1939 (BOOK OF)
BMW M/CYCLES R26 R27 (1956-1967) FACTORY WSM
BMW M/CYCLES R50 R50S R60 R69S (1955-1969) FACTORY WSM
BSA BANTAM (BOOK OF)
BSA ALL FOUR-STROKE SINGLES & V-TWINS 1936-1952 (BOOK OF)
BSA OHV & SV SINGLES - 250cc 1954-1970 (BOOK OF)
BSA OHV & SV SINGLES 1945-54 250-600cc (BOOK OF)
BSA OHV SINGLES 350 & 500cc 1955-1967 (BOOK OF)
BSA PRE-WAR MODELS TO 1939 (BOOK OF)
BSA TWINS 1948-1962 (BOOK OF)
BSA TWINS 1962-1969 (SECOND BOOK OF)
CATALOG OF BRITISH MOTORCYCLES (1951 MODELS)
DOUGLAS PRE-WAR ALL MODELS 1929-1939 (BOOK OF)
DOUGLAS POST-WAR ALL MODELS 1948-1957 FACTORY WSM
DUCATI 160cc, 250cc & 350cc OHC MODELS FACTORY WSM
HONDA 50 ALL MODELS UP TO 1970 INC MONKEY & TRAIL (BOOK OF)
HONDA 90 ALL MODELS UP TO 1966 (BOOK OF)
HONDA MOTORCYCLES 125-150 TWINS C/CS/CB/CA WSM
HONDA MOTORCYCLES 250-305 TWINS C/CS/CB WSM
HONDA MOTORCYCLES C100 SUPER CUB WSM
HONDA MOTORCYCLES C110 SPORT CUB 1962-1969 WSM
HONDA TWINS & SINGLES 50cc TO 305cc 1960-1966 (BOOK OF)
HONDA TWINS ALL MODELS 125cc THRU 450cc UP TO 1968 (BOOK OF)
LAMBRETTA ALL 125 & 150cc MODELS 1947-1957 (BOOK OF)
LAMBRETTA LI & TV MODELS 1957-1970 (SECOND BOOK OF)
MATCHLESS 350 & 500cc SINGLES 1945-1956 (BOOK OF)
MATCHLESS 350 & 500cc SINGLES 1955-1966 (BOOK OF)
NORTON 1938-1956 (BOOK OF)
NORTON DOMINATOR TWINS 1955-1965 (BOOK OF)
NORTON MOTORCYCLES 1957-1970 FACTORY WSM
NORTON PRE-WAR MODELS 1932-1939 (BOOK OF)
ROYAL ENFIELD 736cc INTERCEPTOR FACTORY WSM
ROYAL ENFIELD 250cc & 350cc SINGLES 1958-1966 (SECOND BOOK OF)
SUZUKI 50cc & 80cc UP TO 1966 (BOOK OF)
SUZUKI T10 1963-1967 FACTORY WSM
SUZUKI T20 & T200 1965-1969 FACTORY WSM
TRIUMPH PRE-WAR MOTORCYCLE 1935-1939 (BOOK OF)
TRIUMPH MOTORCYCLES 1937-1951 WSM
TRIUMPH MOTORCYCLES 1941-1955 FACTORY WSM
TRIUMPH TWINS 1956-1969 (BOOK OF)
VELOCETTE ALL SINGLES & TWINS 1925-1970 (BOOK OF)
VESPA 1951-1961 (BOOK OF)
VINCENT MOTORCYCLES 1935-1955 WSM

www.VelocePress.com

www.ingramcontent.com/pod-product-compliance
Lightning Source LLC
Chambersburg PA
CBHW081925170426
43200CB00014B/2830